REWIRE YOUR BRAIN

How to Calm your Anxious Brain.

Stop Fear, Worry, and Anger.

Change your Habits for a Better Life.

JAMES RULES

Table of Contents

Introduction

The unused potential of your brain is huge!
Do you feel a lack of:

• success

• luck

• joy

• satisfaction

• health

• self-confidence

• material benefits

One tip: **rewire your mind!** Essentially, this means developing intelligence. In other words, giving yourself a much-needed upgrade. A small reservation: there is no hint that your level of intelligence is lower than that of others. The fact is that practically all people have intelligence that works well below the level of their real capabilities!

The unused potential of the human brain is huge. Imagine: most people use less than ten percent of their brain! In addition, while many of them live very well, do not complain about a lack of intelligence, do a good job with everyday life tasks, and sometimes succeed. What will happen if you start using the potential of the brain not by ten, but at least twenty to thirty percent? You can become a real genius or, at least, the owner of an outstanding mind, an extraordinary person capable of reaching unprecedented heights in science, art, business, politics and in general in any type of activity of your choice.

The higher the intelligence, the less the likelihood of errors, the greater the chance of the best solutions.

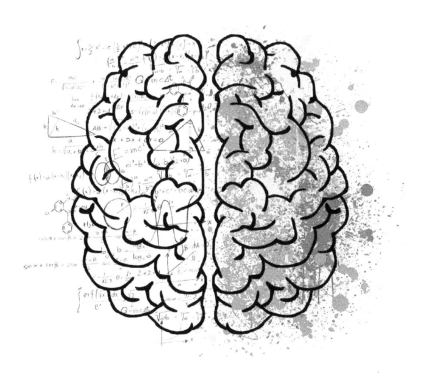

Chapter 1. Rewiring the brain? What is involved?

We live in an amazing time of discovery! Yes, the human brain is still a *terra incognita* ("unknown land") to a large extent. And yet today we know about the functioning of the brain much more than yesterday. Do you know why the brain of different people in different ways assimilates and processes information from the surrounding world? It turns out that this is due to the fact that each person has three main channels of perception of information - **visual, auditory, and kinesthetic** ("sensory").

Someone well perceives visual information, and auditory and kinesthetic - someone, on the contrary, learns everything very well by ear, but does not notice the details of visual images, and someone sees and hears well, but does not understand in the "voice" of sensations. Yes, it is these three sensory channels that create for each of us our own, unique picture of the world! But here they are only developed in most people unevenly. People, which is dominated by the visual channel, called **visuals**, auditory - **audial**, touch - **kinesthetic**.

Note that this is not about any violations in the work of the senses! A person may not suffer from deafness or short-sightedness at all, but still not absorb half of the information that is transmitted through the channels of hearing or vision. As a result, his picture of the world turns out to be incomplete or even distorted. Accordingly, he draws the wrong conclusions - and makes the wrong decisions because he is guided by insufficient or distorted information. Success once again eludes!

Findings:

• it is necessary to develop all three main channels of perception of information

• it is necessary to learn to process information coming through all three channels correctly

• need to be able to draw conclusions and make decisions based on the complete information

The manual, which you hold in your hands, is intended for training intelligence. But this is an unusual training - it takes into account the **individual characteristics** of the brain of each person. If you follow all the recommendations of the book and do the exercises, then:

• the capabilities of your intellect will grow several times in a short time!

• you will start to feel like a person who has a super modern computer instead of a clerical account!

• having worked your sensory channels, you will instantly solve problems that have not been solved for years!

• You will easily and quickly find answers to all your questions! But these are far from all the benefits that you will get by passing a unique training on the rewiring of the three sensory channels!

In the book, you will find exercises that will help you:

• know yourself better, begin to fully use your abilities and even develop new talents

• use your leading information perception channel even more actively and with the best results

• develop those perception channels that are not actively working for you, and make your picture of the world more complete and vivid

• Instantly assimilate and analyze all information coming through three channels

• improve memory

• increase the ability to learn, understand and learn new information

• catch the necessary information "on the fly."

• be perfectly oriented in any situation

• increase the speed of reaction in any situation - instantly draw the right conclusions and make the best decisions, thus moving from success to success

All that is required of you is to carefully read and do the exercises, spending at least ten minutes a day to do it.

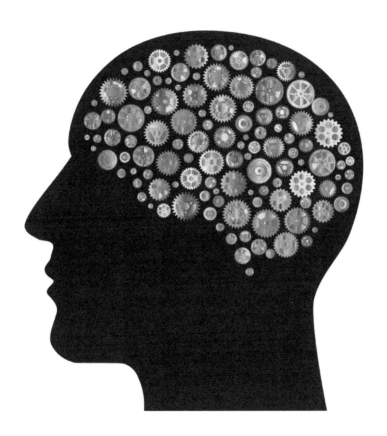

Chapter 2. How your brain works - What determines the style and quality of your thinking?

The world around us is incredibly diverse. There is a huge amount of "food" for our senses - how much we can see, hear, touch, and feel. Sometimes it seems to us that all peoples diversified perception of the world is equally the same. After all, the picture of the world seems objective to us, and we think that other people see, hear, touch, and feel the same as we do. Actually, it is not. Each person perceives the world in his own way. We can say that our senses and our brain create a kind of "filters" or "lenses" through which we perceive the world.

So, other people can see, hear, and feel is not the same as you!

One person enjoys a beautiful sunset, and the other does not even notice it. Someone enjoys music, but to another, it annoys her. One is important that the clothes are comfortable, and the other is easily put up with the inconvenience, if only it was beautiful. Someone does not remember the faces but remembers the details of the conversation, and someone - vice versa. Some people like to read; others like to listen to audiobooks.

Comparisons can be continued; they are almost endless. The bottom line is that all people in varying degrees perceive three types of signals from the outside world – visual, auditory, and "sensory" (kinesthetic) signals. However, each of these ways of perception is developed in different people in different ways. Usually, only one of these three types of perception is leading, the second type is developed to a lesser extent, and the third type is developed quite weakly.

There is no person who by nature, all three types of perception would be equally developed! So, one of us is primarily visual, someone is auditory, and someone is kinesthetic. Representatives of each of these types live as if in three different worlds!

The visual perceives first of all that which can be seen with the eyes. His world is first of all the world of visual images. He best remembers and assimilates visual information.

The audial perceive the world more at the hearing. His world is a world of sounds, words, speech. What he sees is assimilated and remembered by him to a lesser extent.

Kinesthetic perceives the world through feelings and sensations. It is important for him to touch everything, "feel the skin," or feel it through muscle feeling and other bodily sensations. All other information seems insufficient to him.

According to statistics, forty percent of all people are visuals, another forty percent are kinesthetic, and only twenty percent of humanity are audials.

"Distortion" in the direction of one of the three ways of perception is not at all some pathology, not a violation, not a deviation from the norm. We are all different, and this is the norm. It is just that each person has his own style and quality of thinking, and this is connected with the prevailing type of perception, with which sensory channel is the leading one. But this does not mean that it is impossible to develop those ways of perception that you have developed to a lesser extent. On the contrary, it is possible and necessary to develop them. The more fully you have developed all types of perception, the closer you are to harmony.

The map of the brain can change, which means that intellectual abilities can increase!

The brain creates a picture of the world, passing its images through the senses: visual images through the eyes, auditory images through the ears. As for kinesthetic perception, it does not envisage the nature of a single sense organ: kinesthetic perception of the world is carried out both through touch, smell and taste, and through the vestibular apparatus, as well as special bodily sensations, such as muscle feeling, temperature and pain sensations, sense of movement, tension, and relaxation, heaviness, and lightness, "goosebumps", etc.

The differences in perception are not related to the state of health of the sense organs. A shortsighted person can be a wonderful visual, and one who has a hearing loss due to illness will not cease to be audial if he was one before. It is not so much about the sense organs as such, but about how the brain analyzes and perceives the information coming in through them.

Information from the outside world (and not only from the outside but from the internal environment of the body) comes primarily to the receptors - these are special cells whose function is precisely to respond to certain stimuli. As soon as the stimulus has hit the receptors, a chemical reaction immediately takes place in them. As a result, energy is released, which is transmitted to the nerve. The nerve is nothing but the fibers of neurons, nerve cells, which are the main elements of the nervous system. The nerve transmits the received information to neurons, then it is transmitted further to other, third neurons, and finally reaches the part of the brain where recognition and analysis of this information take place, and a reaction to it in the form of certain sensations is born.

*On how exactly the corresponding area of the brain is organized, it just depends on how complete the perception and assimilation of this information will be. If this is a **developed area**, with many neural connections, forming a stable neural network - then the information will be perceived and assimilated in the best way. If this is, let's say, an **insufficiently trained part of the** brain, where neural connections are unstable and not enough - some of the information may go unnoticed, and the picture of the world will suffer significant damage!*

The more actively in our nerve cells, the neurons work more, the richer the neural networks they create, resulting from the interaction of neurons. Each neural network creates a kind of program that guides our skills, abilities, perception, and analysis of information. Thus, systems are created in the brain that is responsible for each of our functions and actions. The combination of these systems, scientists call the **brain map**. According to this map, the whole brain can be said to be divided into **zones**, or **regions**, each with its own function. The ability to perceive sound is assigned to a specific zone. Light, color, and the visual images they create are the prerogatives of another brain area. A separate zone is also responsible for the kinesthetic sensations.

How we perceive the corresponding signals from the outside world depends on the development of the brain areas responsible for them.

Why are they not developed in the majority of people? It is hard to say - after all, the brain is still far from being fully studied by scientists; in many ways, it remains a mystery to science! Surely heredity, and the experience gained in infancy, and education, are factors. But there are other, still unexplained factors that determine why we become visuals, audials, or kinesthetics. One thing is clear: each person has his strengths and weaknesses in the perception of reality. And we must learn to use our strengths to the full - and develop the weakest ones by training.

The fact that such development is possible at any age is confirmed by practice. And modern science provides a rationale for the fact that brain training brings great results. After all, if only recently it was believed that the map of the human brain is unchanged, today scientists come to completely different conclusions: the map of the brain can change!

Otherwise, how can one explain the fact that a person whose brain area responsible for sound perception is damaged as a result of injury or illness can learn to hear again after some time? The other site took over the functions of the damaged ones, as there were formed new connections between the neurons instead of the missing ones. The brain map has changed; the brain has re-learned the impaired function.

Recent studies by scientists have revealed such an amazing thing: the brain area that processes visual information is able to perceive and analyze sound signals. It is thanks to this that we can create visual images in our imagination when we hear speech or music. Sounds are transformed into visual images thanks to the same area of the brain responsible for the auditory information! And the more we train in creating such images - visualization, the better this area of the brain works. Similarly, we can train our brain to perceive any information - visual, sound, kinesthetic better.

As you train, the brain will create new neural networks and improve existing ones. As a result, our picture of the world will become more complete; we will no longer pass important information past us, which means that the work of our intellect will be much more productive than before.

Consider: what is more in your picture of the world - visual images, sounds, sensations? Do you perceive the world brightly and fully? Doesn't it happen that you don't notice something important, skip past the ears or don't react to the signals that the body sends (it sometimes gives us not less important information than the one that is visible to the eyes and heard by the ears)? On the basis of incomplete or misunderstood information, we inevitably draw wrong conclusions and make wrong decisions. That is why you need to develop your brain map, training it for full-fledged visual, auditory, and kinesthetic perception.

Chapter 3. Start thinking three times more efficiently!

And now, about the most important thing. Our type of perception depends on the style and quality of our thinking. We can say that visual thinking is peculiar to the visual, the audial to the auditory, kinesthetic to the kinesthetic. What does it mean?

The visual perceive any problem and task through visual images. He *sees the* problem. In addition, he also needs to *see the* decision - literally, in the form of a clear and precise picture, even if it is imaginary, even if it reflects the desired future, but he needs exactly the picture. If he does not see a picture corresponding to his solved problem, realized desire, or achieved the goal - he is unlikely to be able to get what he wants.

The audial perceives all vital tasks, mainly through hearing. Facing a problem, he wants to *hear* as much as possible in connection with it. In addition, how to solve the problem, he needs to *hear.*

Kinesthetic guided by feeling. He *feels the* problems and, before solving them, must *feel* how the problem can be solved.

Thus, not only the analysis, perception of the world, each person approaches from the point of view of his leading style of thinking - but also the solution of problems and tasks, the construction of his life, the creation of something new in it. The visual recreates his visual images in reality, the audial - what he heard and voiced, kinesthetic embodies into reality what he could feel, feel even without words and pictures.

Can you imagine how good it would be if we could both see and hear, and feel the problem and its solution? We would have learned three times more about the problem and how to solve it! Moreover, most importantly, we would get three times more opportunities to realize our desires, achieve goals; that is, we would have three times more ways to success!

This is precisely the purpose of this manual - to develop to the maximum extent all three types of thinking: visual, auditory, and kinesthetic.

Further work: from theory to practice

At this point, we end up with the theory and proceed to practice.

The following chapters:

• By external signs to determine whom you are - visual, audial or kinetics;

• be tested and make more accurate conclusions about the prevailing sensory channel.

Carefully read all the following materials and be sure to complete all the proposed tasks. Only after that, it will be possible to proceed to the following chapter - the actual training of the intellect.

Signs to help you know who you are - visual, audial, or kinesthetic

Introspection: What do you remember first?

Remember some meaningful or just a pleasant, memorable event from your life. What is remembered first - what you saw, what you heard, or what you felt?

Each event is stored in memory in the form of a certain set of images. These are visual images reflecting what you saw, auditory images formed from the sounds surrounding you, and kinesthetic images based on the experienced sensations. After analyzing which images prevail when you try to remember an event, you can understand which category you belong to - are you a visual, audial or kinesthetic.

Did you immediately "see" a bright picture in your imagination? This is a sign of a visual. Poorly remember the picture, but the sounds, voices, and spoken words were well imprinted in the memory? This is a characteristic feature of the audience. Sounds and visual images are vaguely remembered but do you remember well your own sensations - heat or cold, relaxation or tone, vigor or fatigue, and also remember the smells perfectly? The chances are good that you are kinesthetic.

If it is still difficult for you to determine what type you are, take a paper and a pen and, without thinking, describe any situation in your life. Not necessarily in detail - you can restrict brief phrases. Write what comes to mind; do not think too much about the wording. Re-read, paying attention to the definitions. Do they refer to visual, auditory, or kinesthetic imagery?

Different people will describe the same situation in different ways. For example.

Option 1. Blue sea, high mountains covered with green forest, bright pink sunset, snow-white seagulls soar in the azure sky among white clouds.

Option 2. Loud cries of seagulls, the roar of the sea surf, the rustling of the wind in the branches, the distant echo in the mountains - nothing more breaks the silence.

Option 3. Affectionate, warm sea waves, stones heated by the sun, clean air, which is so pleasant to breathe deeply.

Undoubtedly, you have already understood that option 1 belongs to the visual, option 2 to the audials, option 3 to kinesthetics.

Chapter 4. Exercise complexes

From the previous chapters you found out:
• Which sensory channel is your master channel - that is, the one you use most often?
• Which sensory channel is your second after - that is, the one you use sometimes;
• Which sensory channel is the least developed in you that is one that you rarely or never use.

Further practical material is built so that you can:
• First, improve the channel that you use most often - to learn how to use it more effectively;
• To master the most effective ways to learn and assimilate information for your leading channel;
• Then develop those channels that you use only occasionally;
• After that, engage in the development of channels that you almost never use;
• and at the end of the work on the book, you will perform exercises for the development of visual, auditory, and kinesthetic memory, intended for all readers, regardless of which sensory channels they dominate.

The following three chapters are designed to work with your activity type.

Chapter 5 - exercises for visuals.

Chapter 6 - exercises for audials.

Chapter 7 - exercises for kinesthetics.

Having determined which channel you have is the most used and active, select from the three chapters, the one that relates to this channel and performs all the exercises sequentially.

This is necessary to make your strengths even stronger. It would seem what is the point - because the strengths are already strong. However, the fact is that to have a strong side is one thing, but to be able to use it is completely different.

The ability of a visual, audial, or kinesthetic is akin to talent. In order for talent to bear fruit, it is necessary, firstly, to learn about it, secondly, to develop it and, thirdly, to apply it in practice.

After all, if you are, for example, a visual, then you best assimilate information that comes in a visual, visible form. Consequently, having learned to isolate visual signals in the surrounding information environment accurately and instantly analyze them, you will repeatedly increase your thinking abilities and begin to orient yourself much more effectively in all situations, quickly and more accurately understand what is happening, make the right conclusions and make the right decisions.

The same applies to audials and kinesthetics - by isolating audio signals and kinesthetic signals that are close and comprehensible to themselves, they will also begin to live and think much more efficiently. For this, you need training. Thanks to it, you will learn how to use better your natural abilities, which means to make the best and most correct decisions, to act more efficiently, to achieve success in anything and more easily and quickly to solve the most complex problems. Moreover, all thanks to the fact that you are thinking will become perfect.

Each chapter consists of the following sections:

• Exercises for the development of care;

• Exercises for the mental reconstruction of visual, auditory or kinesthetic images;

• Exercise on the work of the imagination - the creation, creative design of relevant images;

• exercises that train the skill of "translating" information coming through less developed channels into the "language" that you understand - images corresponding to your leading channel;

• Exercises to help solve problems;

• Exercises that help in achieving success.

Attention is the most important factor in shaping the strength and effectiveness of your intellect. Many people do not know how to think effectively simply because they are absent-minded and inattentive. In the section of each chapter devoted to attention, you will master the exercises, thanks to which you will not miss the visual, auditory, or kinesthetic signals that are important for you.

Creating visual, auditory, kinesthetic images trains the creative, creative possibilities of your mind. The only one who thinks creatively can find the best solution to any task and is able to generate ideas leading from success to success.

"Translation" of any information into a "language" that you understand (for example, visual images — into sensations, sounds — into pictures, etc.) is a skill that will help you to catch much more signals from the surrounding reality and understand them much better to make more correct conclusions and act more effectively.

Problem-solving involves actively using your lead channel first to see it, hear or feel it most fully, and because of this, turn on the intellect to its fullest to figure out, draw conclusions, and then again see, hear, or feel the solution using your lead channel and bring it to life. Also in this section, you will learn how to get rid of unwanted memories, problems stretching from the past, to improve your mood and psychological state, to get at your disposal more strength and energy.

Achieving success will cease to be a problem when you use your leading channel at full power and, as a result, all the power of intelligence. In this section, your abilities are used both to reproduce and to create visual, auditory, or kinesthetic images. You will learn how to create your own way of success and customize your mind for its realization.

Every reader needs to go through only one of the chapters 5, 6, and 7- at least for a start. After completing all the exercises in the chapter on training your active type of perception, you can proceed to the next chapters.

How to do the exercises?

How often to do the exercises?

Desirable every day. Just one exercise per day is enough. If you have time and desire, you can do two or three exercises a day. No longer, need not to overdo it.

How many times to do each exercise?

As much as you want. If you feel that from the first time not everything worked out, as you would like, repeat it again. You cannot immediately but after a break. You can repeat the next day and every other day. Clear rules do not exist here. It all depends on your desire.

What time to do the exercises?

It is undesirable to perform most exercises immediately before bedtime - otherwise, you can fall asleep during the exercise or, conversely, the exercise will prevent sleep. As soon as you wake up, it is also better not to do it, since exercises, as a rule, require an active state of consciousness. Otherwise, there are no restrictions - work at any time of the day convenient for you.

Chapter 5. Exercises for visuals

Exercise **"Unnoticed details"**
It happens that even a pronounced visual does not notice the details and the details of the environment only because of haste, inattention, and habit to look, not seeing. Therefore, attention exercises are an important stage in training visual abilities.

Pick up a small object that is often in front of your eyes - for example, a cup, a vase, a pencil stand, a desk clock, or even a mobile phone. Maybe you think that the appearance of this item is familiar to you. Set a goal to find in it at least ten details that you have not previously paid attention to. Notice even tiny scratches, barely noticeable chips, as well as the shape and color of various small elements.

Exercise "New look at the old house."

After leaving the street, devote at least 5–10 minutes to carefully examine your own house or any other well-known building. Do you know what windows and doors look like; do you know all the details of the facade, the shape of the roof, and what you can see on it? Look at the house with a fresh look, and it will seem to you that you have not seen it for a long time, although you look every day.

Exercise "Apples"

Pick up an apple or any other fruit and carefully consider it. Note what color it is, shape. How correct is the form? How do shades of color go from one to another? What features does this apple have - maybe specks or irregularities?

Take another apple and consider it. Then compare the two apples, finding as many differences as possible. Formulate these differences aloud, trying to select the most accurate words as possible.

Exercise "Familiar faces."

How long have you not just looked at people close and familiar to you, but really saw them? Most people do not really look at familiar faces, because they believe that they know them so well. As a result, they communicate not with real people, but with their own idea of these people, with a long-established image. But this image is constantly changing, although sometimes imperceptibly.

Peer at faces that seem familiar and known to you for a long time. You can do it gradually, imperceptibly. Set a goal to find new, unfamiliar features, changes that you have not noticed. You can expect new discoveries - you will better know and understand loved ones.

Exercises to develop the ability to reproduce visual images

Exercise "Picture of the day."

This exercise should be performed in the evening, but not before bedtime, but at least two or three hours before bedtime. Sit or lie down in a comfortable position, do not close your eyes.

Start to remember everything that you saw during the day, trying not to miss the little things and details. Start right from the moment you wake up: remember what you saw when you opened your eyes, then what items were in front of your eyes, when you got up and did the usual morning procedures, when you had breakfast, got ready for work, then what you saw on the way to work, and etc. up to the present moment.

Scroll your day before your eyes, like a movie, and from time to time like a picture to stop to see it in detail. For example, remember what people you met, what hairstyles they were dressed in. Do you think you have enough details? On the other hand, paid attention only to the fact that itself was conspicuous?

Were there any moments during the day when the visual images seemed to blur and dim, and you cannot recall them in detail? What do you think it is connected with? Maybe you are tired or too busy with your thoughts. Try these moments as if to scroll in slow motion, so that you will still remember some details.

Then scroll the same "movie," only in the opposite direction: from the present moment to the beginning of the day. Maybe you will be able to remember something that you missed during the first "viewing."

Pay attention: your "film" should contain only visual images - try to exclude sounds and sensations from your perception.

Exercise "Favorite place."

Imagine yourself in a place that you like. This may be a place where you like to relax, spend your vacation or just one of your favorite places in any part of the world, and maybe even near you're home.

Eyes for this exercise can be closed, but if you prefer to perform with your eyes open - do so.

Imagine that you are in this place. Imagine everything that you see around, in the smallest detail. If you do not remember any of the details, you can mummify them. Carefully consider this mental picture, trying not to miss anything. Imagine that you really are there - "see" everything as a reality.

Exercise "Objects"

Without closing your eyes, alternately imagine any objects - those that you cannot see around you, and you can only imagine. Let it be all that comes to your head, do not hesitate too much, just call the first word that came to your head and immediately draws the corresponding visual image, for example, birch, suitcase, coat, iceberg, sun, car, etc.

For a long time, do not linger on each image, but try to present them as clearly as possible, clearly and in detail.

Exercise "Creativity with objects." Imagine what you see in front of you. A set of objects - any, which first come to mind, no less than five or seven. Let it be completely unrelated items. Your task is to connect them in your imagination so that you get some kind of holistic picture (for example, a still life). Do not rush, combine objects in this way, and that way, carefully visualizing the very process of manipulation with them.

No need to look for practical application of what you get - your task is to create a holistic picture that will be akin to a work of art. For example, your set is a candle, a rope, a flower, an anchor, a bicycle. You can consistently imagine how to tie a bicycle with a rope with an anchor, and stick a flower into a candle and place this composition somewhere on the steering wheel or saddle. What is not an installation?

There is no limit to the imagination, but the main thing is to present the objects themselves as clearly as possible, and what you do with them, and what you end up with.

Exercise "Imaginary Apple"

You do not need to close your eyes during this exercise. Imagine that in front of you is an apple on a plate. Consider both an imaginary plate and an imaginary apple, imagining that you actually see it. What is the size and color of the plate? Is there a drawing on it? What size, color, the shape is an apple? Imagine an apple turning with a plate. You do not touch it, just looking from all sides. Does it look the same from different angles or differently? What are the differences?

Now imagine that the apple is moving away, decreasing in size. Then again approaching, and so on several times. Watch carefully for resizing.

Then imagine that the apple rises above the level of your eyes, then goes down, then moves to the right, then to the left. Mentally watch what an apple looks like at this change in the angle of view.

Now imagine that in the room where you are, the lights go out slowly. How does the image of an apple change, what happens to its color, contours? Suddenly the light flashes very brightly. What does an apple look like now? Then darkness comes sharply. Do you see an apple? If so, how does it look? Do you distinguish the contours, shape, and color? Your eyes gradually get used to the dark. What does an apple look like now?

Then imagine that normal lighting is restored in the room. Look at the apple again.

Achieve the brightness and clarity of perception of the image throughout the exercise.

Exercises to create visual images

Exercise "Imaginary renovation of the home."

Close your eyes and imagine that the room in which you live — a room, an apartment, or a whole house — remains completely empty. You have to re-arrange the interior. Your task is to make the home as updated as possible. Let the new interior be completely different from the old one. Decide what color and texture will be the walls, ceiling, floor, what furniture and how you arrange in a renewable room. It is important not only to decide but also to imagine all this as clearly as possible, in detail and in detail. If you are visual, you have a well-developed spatial vision. Nevertheless, you can develop it even more. This will help you in implementing a variety of your plans.

If it seems to you that your existing home is too crowded for the flight of your imagination, imagine a new house or apartment. Imagine how you equip this new home from scratch. "See" with your mind's eye the whole picture. Do not forget about the details, the smallest details - such as, for example, curbs and baseboards, lamps, paintings on the walls, pillows on the couch, napkins and tablecloths, bedspreads, soft toys, figurines, dishes in the closet, etc.

Mentally change the options for decoration and design until the interior does not seem complete and perfect. Practice until you "see" the picture as bright, clear, and visible as in reality.

Exercise "Mental Transformation"

Imagine any small object — for example, the same apple, cup, vase, mobile phone, pencil, etc. It is important that this is an imaginary object — that is, there must not be a corresponding real object before your eyes.

Eyes do not need to close. With open eyes, look at an imaginary object in front of you as if it were real.

Your task is to mentally produce a series of transformations of the object, changing its color, shape, size, but not the essence. That is, the apple should remain an apple, and the cup should remain a cup. Let these objects, remaining what they are, change in your imagination all their possible characteristics. If this is a cup, then its material can also change (for example, from porcelain it turns into clay), and the color, shape of

---

the handle, etc. If the apple - let it change color, but it must remain the color characteristic of the apple (for example, it cannot be blue, violet, etc.). The more variations of the subject you find, the more clearly you imagine them, the better.

Exercise "Unreal transformation."

Imagine the same subject as in the previous exercise. Now your task is not just to modify it, but mentally turn it into something else. Eyes also do not need to close.

Decide what exactly you will turn the subject. Any transformations are allowed, including the transformation of the non-living into the living and vice versa. For example, you presented a cup and want to turn it into a cat. The only condition is that the transformation should be gradual. That is, it is impossible to go straight from the cup to the cat. First, mentally change the shape of the cup so that it becomes a figurine depicting a cat. To do this, gradually change the shape of the cup so that, for example, the handle turns into a tail, and the cup itself slowly, smoothly acquires the outlines of a cat's body. Bring the statuette to perfection, and then you can "revive" it - also slowly, gradually, watching the fur, mustache, claws on the paws, etc. appear. The more stages of the transformation process you go through, the better.

Think up and mentally implement several options for turning various objects into others.

Exercise "Repaint the landscape."

Imagine any landscape that is preserved in your memory. If it is difficult to remember something, imagine the picture outside the window. Eyes do not need to close. Imagine that you mentally repaint the landscape. The colors you can use are the most fantastic. For example, the mountains can be painted in mauve color; the sea - in yellow, the sky - is green, etc.

Imagine how the whole picture will look like after repainting. Change colors at will five or six times in a row. Then mentally return the landscape to its natural state.

Exercise "Perfect Place"

Mentally transfer to any place that you like - absolutely real, where you have already been. Imagine that all the colors have become much brighter than they really are. Mentally add more light, as if all things and objects shine. Carefully consider how the look of a familiar place has changed.

Think about what else you would like to improve in this picture. Indeed, in the real world, there is no perfection, but in your imagination, you can create the perfect world you can dream of. Give your favorite corner the ideal properties that are not in reality. Enjoy your stay in the place of your dreams, even if it has turned completely into the fruit of your imagination.

Thus, you can mentally experiment with any places, things, and objects, improving them, as you want.

Legacy Exercise

Imagine that you inherited a large old apartment, and perhaps a manor or even a palace, a castle - everything depends on your imagination. Imagine that you came there for the first time and saw a lot of rooms filled with old things. At first, you just go and look at them. Present in detail all you can see there. Then take a closer look at the fine details - interior decoration, furniture, paintings, etc. Imagine that you pick up the items that interest you most and look at them.

Then imagine what you are looking into cabinets, drawers. What do you see there? Maybe you found a chest or a box and open them too. Imagine every object that can be found there. Imagine it in detail.

Exercise "Airplane"

Imagine that you are standing on the top of a mountain and look at the sky. The sky is blue, clear. A plane flies high in the sky. Behind him stretches trail in the form of a white stripe. Imagine as clearly as possible the blue of the sky, the plane, and the train.

Imagine that you, while on the ground, can mentally control the flight of an airplane. Imagine that at your will, the plane begins to perform aerobatics. You send it up and down, following him with your eyes. He moves along the most bizarre trajectories.

Then let the plane, according to your will, draw some figure in the sky - for example, a figure eight. Imagine how he describes the corresponding figure and a white mark in the form of the eight remains in the sky. It gradually melts and dissolves in the sky. Now let the plane write some letter. Also, watch how it appears and melts in the sky. Then think up some word that the plane should write. This could be, for example, your name, the name of your city, or just any word you like. Imagine how the plane writes it in the sky, and then it slowly dissolves.

You can even write a whole phrase, such as a declaration of love to someone or a desire that you would like to fulfill.

Exercise "Behind the Turn"

Imagine what is behind the bend of your street or the road you are driving. Imagine that you were behind this turn. What do you see and what do you think is happening there? What kind of cars go, what kind of pedestrians are they, what are they wearing, etc.

Having trained in this, try at an opportunity to imagine what is happening around the corner, where you have not been. For example, you walk, and you have to turn the corner. Imagine what you see there. Do not be surprised if you eventually learn quite accurately to predict the picture, even for completely unfamiliar turns.

Exercise "Imaginary animal."

Come up with an imaginary animal - what does not exist in nature. Dragons, unicorns, centaurs do not fit - although they are unreal creatures, someone before you already invented them. Your task is to create in your imagination, a creature that was not created by anyone before you.

Draw it in your imagination in detail. Is it big or small, with smooth skin or covered with hair, what are his eyes, ears, tail, and teeth? Is it predatory, dangerous, wild or innocuous, homemade? What goals can this animal serve? Can it be a means of transportation? Can I hunt him? Alternatively, maybe it is decorative. On the other hand, live in the wild, serving as a decoration of the landscape? How can you communicate with him? Can I iron it, feed it with my hand, or is it better to keep at a safe distance?

Imagine all this as a reality. Imagine yourself a participant in a "movie" where you are a hero who communicates with a given animal invented by you.

Come up with a name for this animal, and if you want, then the name.

Exercise "Imaginary Opening Day"

Imagine that you are on an opening day. The exposition is located in several rooms. The idea of the exhibition organizers is such that in the first hall there are only paintings in red, in the second - in orange, in the third - in yellow, in the fourth - in green, in the fifth - in blue, in the sixth - in blue, in the seventh - in purple, and in the eighth hall are seven paintings, each of which correspond to one of the seven colors of the rainbow.

Imagine that you alternately go through all the halls of the opening day, carefully examining the paintings in each of them. What scenes do you think fit each color? Imagine the pictures as clearly, clearly, and in detail as possible. It can picture not only completely created by your imagination but also real-life canvases, already seen by you, only with a modified color gamut. Can you, for example, imagine a picture of "The Ninth Wave" in orange shades?

Exercise "Sculptor"

Imagine that you are a sculptor who needs to cut a statue out of a huge piece of marble. Think of what kind of statue it will be. "See" her with your mind's eye. You must clearly and clearly see in your imagination the future result of your creation. A true artist is capable of presenting his future work in exactly this way - as if it already exists. First, "seeing" the result with his mind's eye, then later he embodies it in his work.

Imagine that you, too, clearly know what you want to get in the end. Imagine the smallest details - the texture of marble, its drawing, all the features and forms of the future sculpture.

Then again, imagine what you see in front of you a block of marble. In addition, imagine it also in every detail - color, texture, shape, size, and pattern. Then imagine how you start to work and gradually begin to cut off unnecessary from the stone. It does not matter if you are unfamiliar with the technology of the sculptor - imagine that unnecessary pieces of marble are cut off by themselves, according to your desire or the wave of your hand. Gradually turn a block of marble into the desired sculpture and bring it to perfection.

Exercise "Director"

Imagine that you are a director and you have to make a film on any literary work. To get started, take a little story. As you read it, imagine all the images, scenes, pictures as vividly as possible. Do not hurry, think out even what the writer has disregarded - for example, the details of the interior and the costumes of the characters, the landscape, the surrounding objects.

Choose actors for your movie. It does not have to be famous actors - you can imagine any people in place of heroes if you think that they are suitable for these roles. In addition, you can imagine completely unfamiliar people.

Reading each line, imagine watching a movie, not reading a book. Let the pictures of this film unfold before your inner sight. Think over the colors and the general atmosphere - is it bright, joyful or muffled, gloomy, with a hint of drama? You will feel how color and image is connected with perception, with emotional mood.

Ensure that your "film" appears in your imagination as clearly and clearly as possible.

Exercise "Journey to the inside of the picture."

Look carefully at any picture you like - in a museum, at an exhibition or at a reproduction. Then imagine that you are stepping inside a picture - and you are on the other side of the objects depicted on it.

What do they look like from the other side? Draw in your imagination as clearly as possible visual images. Imagine bypassing objects from different angles. If people are depicted in the picture - also imagine how they look, for example, from the back of the head, or from the side - in a view that is not visible, if you look at the canvas like an ordinary viewer. Imagine that you look around the inside of the picture. Feel the volume of space and all items.

Then try to look behind the frame of the picture mentally. What do you think is left there? Are there any objects, things that the artist could see, but left them outside the picture? Expand the picture in your imagination to the maximum possible limits.

Now imagine yourself as a character picture. What would you look like? What would you be wearing? What pose would take?

Treat this exercise as a game. You can be inside the picture for as long as you like, viewing what is depicted there, from different sides and even acting as a character. When you get tired of this, just imagine that you leave the picture and return to real life.

Exercises to help translate sounds and sensations in visual images

Exercise "Sound and Picture"

This exercise is intended for visuals who have difficulty perceiving the world through other channels. You can always "translate" information into your own "language" at the right time, and then it will become much clearer to you. To do this, you can use the method of associations - to represent what kind of visible image associated with certain images, such as sounds and sensations.

At first, we will try to translate sounds into colors. Imagine one by one the sounds described below and, without really thinking, call aloud what color or shade of color they associate with you. Keep in mind: there are no right or wrong answers because the associations for each person can be individual and are connected precisely with his peculiarities of perception. If one person has a ticking clock associated with yellow, another has a white one, and a third has a blue one, this is normal. It is important for you to find your own association, which will help make the beep more distinct for you.

So, what color do you associate with?

• the sound of a passing car

• knock of heels on asphalt

• kitten meowing

• the growl of a tiger

• alarm bell

• the sound of a light breeze

• strong wind noise

- clinking glasses
- the sound of breaking dishes
- nightingale singing
- the sound of a fire siren
- splashing water
- the sound of sea waves
- the crackling of the fire
- the sound of a working drill
- the rustle of book pages
- drumroll
- fan noise
- knock off the metronome
- croaking frog
- cow mooing
- the sound of tearing paper
- clock chime
- bell ringing

Now let's complicate the task: determine the forms with which all these sounds are associated with you. Perhaps some of them seem rounded, others - rectangular, etc.? Again, look for your own associations, without thinking about whether you are "right" or "wrong."

Then you can go even further: find objects, things, phenomena of the surrounding world that you associate with these sounds.

Exercise "Sensation and the picture."

This exercise is similar to the previous one; only now we will translate into visual images, not sounds, but sensations.

First, determine the color with which you associate the following sensations:

• cold

• heat

• frost

• heaviness

• ease

• weightlessness

• the feeling of immersion in water

• breath of fresh air

• a touch of fine silk to the skin

• an apple that you hold in your hand

• touching the rough surface of granite

• dough, which you crush with hands

• touching cold metal

• prickly Christmas needles

Now determine with what forms, volumes these sensations are associated, then - with what objects, things, phenomena.

Problem-solving exercises

Exercise "Visualization problems."

For a visual, the most effective way to solve a problem begins with visualization. The visual should see the problem - only then he will be able to understand its essence properly, and therefore, to see the solution. Often, the problem is not solved precisely because we do not have a clear idea about it - about what, in fact, needs to be done for the problem to be solved. The simplest way to clarify this issue is to imagine the problem in the most understandable images for yourself, for a visual it is visual images.

Think about the problem or problem you would like to solve. For example, you would like to change jobs, but you have doubts, you are not sure that you know exactly what you want. Create for yourself a visual image of your current work. To do this, simply imagine all those visible images that are associated with work for you. The simplest thing: imagine everything that you see when you work, for example, interiors, furniture, things, objects, people's faces, specifically your workplace, etc. Determine what exactly you do not like in these images. Maybe you would like to be in other interiors, have other objects in front of your eyes, see otherwise dressed people? Determine what specifically you would like to see in connection with the work. Create for yourself a new, desired image of work, and it will help you make the right choice.

In the same way, you can deal with any problem: create its visual image, determine what exactly you do not like about it, and replace it with the desired images. Thanks to this, you can understand how to act in reality in order to arrive at the desired solution.

49

Exercise "Visualizing problem solving"

After completing the previous exercise, you determined what you do not like in the current situation and what you would like to change. After this, it is not at all difficult to determine what you would like to receive in return. Replace what you don't like in the imagination with the exact opposite - what you might like. For example, if you do not like the cramped house, you would like a spacious house; I do not like the fact that I have to deal with boring papers at work, perhaps I would have liked to work with beautiful, bright things, etc.

Having realized what you would like, you can create a visual image of the solved problem. Even if you do not know yet how to approach the solution to a problem, you can imagine that the problem has already been solved. Imagine yourself in a situation where the problem is solved, and imagine everything that you will see around you in a given situation (for example, in a new job, in a new house, etc.). Let the picture be as detailed as possible.

Important: create just such an imaginary picture that you like.

You want to get what you want. Think carefully about what it can be, and draw the appropriate visual image. As a result, you will know exactly what you want. And most importantly, you will give your brain the task of solving the problem in exactly the best way for you. Your intellectual and creative abilities will awaken, and it will be easier for you to begin to act in the right direction.

Exercise "Getting rid of unwanted experiences."

Thanks to your talent for visualization, you can learn to cope with a bad mood, get rid of negative experiences, and even throw off the burden of problems stretching from the past.

Think about some situation that upset you, or unpleasant memories, from the influence of which you would like to get rid of. Remember the visual images that accompanied this event. All that you saw was the situation where everything happened, the people who participated in it. First, imagine these images as vivid, detailed, as possible.

Then imagine yourself moving these images away from you. Moving away, they decrease. Now imagine that the images lose their colors, become dull. Then imagine that they lose their sharpness, blur. In addition, finally, melt, disappear altogether.

Notice how your feelings have changed with it. When you "erase" the images that accompany negative experiences, the experiences themselves will disappear, negative emotions will no longer have power over you.

Successful Exercises

Exercise "Positive attitude"

Using visual images, you can at any time create for yourself a positive attitude, get a surge of strength and energy, tune in to work, creativity, success, a state of joy and happiness. To do this, you only need to remember when you have already been in such a state - and mentally reproduce the corresponding picture.

For example, you would like to be in a state where you felt strong and confident.

Close your eyes and remember the situation when you felt like that.

Remember the situation - all the visual images that you perceived at that moment, and which were pleasant for you.

Remember the color and shape of these pleasant, positive images.

Then imagine that the picture becomes brighter as if it added light. All the colors around you gain more saturation. The images themselves become more distinct.

Now start mentally bringing these images closer to you. Imagine that, approaching you, they seem to be increasing in size.

You will notice that a pleasant state of confidence and strength will not only arise among you by itself but will even become even more distinct than before. This is because you have enhanced the positive visual signals that, entering into your brain, allowed it to activate a state of confidence and strength.

In the same way, you can reinforce any positive state - by enhancing the visual images accompanying it.

Exercise "New Image of Yourself"

This exercise is useful when you want to improve something in yourself - for example, in your appearance, character, or habits.

Think about the qualities, habits, or external data that you would like to have. Of course, we must proceed from reality: if you are short, you can hardly dream of becoming a two-meter giant. However, here, for example, to lose weight, improve posture and gait, start looking younger, these are quite achievable goals. The same applies to the character: do not strive to redo completely, to become someone else. Nevertheless, to find some positive qualities, being yourself, is quite realistic: for example, to become more confident, decisive, collected, to get rid of bad habits.

Imagine yourself with all the new positive qualities and traits that you would like to acquire. Visualization will be more successful if you remember those moments of your life when you already showed these qualities (for example, you were successful, you are confident, etc.), and remember how you looked then. Make this image as bright and distinct as possible.

Then imagine yourself with those undesirable properties and qualities that you would like to get rid of (for example, from excess weight, stoop, slowness, lethargy, etc.). First, imagine this picture bright, then gradually make it dull, black and white, and then move it away from you so that it becomes a point. Then, on the spot of this point, imagine a new image of yourself - make it colorful, bright, and large.

More often reproduce this new image in front of your inner eye. Your brain will thus receive the command to begin work on your transformation.

Exercise "Visualization dreams."

This exercise will help you achieve your goals, clarifying the visual presentation of them.

Think about what you would like to achieve, what dream to accomplish. If you still do not know which way to move towards the dream and are not even sure about its feasibility - let it not hurt you. Create an image that can sometimes tell you the path to a dream better than your reasoning on this topic.

53

Close your eyes and imagine that the dream came true. Draw in your imagination, a picture of a dream come true. It is very important to imagine everything that you will see in this situation. It is very important to understand and feel that the picture is pleasant to you. If the picture is pleasant, your brain will guide you along the path to achieving the goal. If in the picture there is at least something unpleasant - remove this unpleasant image and replace it with another, pleasant one.

Put yourself inside the picture. Once again, mentally cast her gaze - how it looks from the inside. Make the picture even brighter. At this point, you are bringing yourself closer to your cherished goal, even if you have not yet taken any real steps to achieve it. Such a visualization, if you do it purposefully and regularly, will help you in planning and implementing such steps.

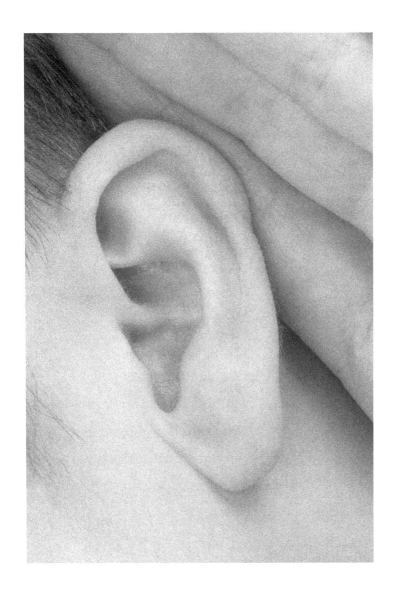

Chapter 6. Exercises for audials

Exercise "Unheard Sounds"

Even an audial can ignore important information from simple carelessness, haste, or lack of listening habits. Therefore, first, it is necessary through training to regain the ability not only to listen but also to hear.

Listen to the sounds, being in the place where you are often, for example, at home. Listen to the sounds inside and outside - in the next room, outside. Call aloud or to yourself all the sounds that you can notice.

Make it your goal to hear everything, even the quietest sounds, including those that you previously didn't pay attention to - perhaps unnoticed shades in the ticking of the clock, a slight rustling of the wind outside the window or the creaking of floorboards in the next room. Count at least ten varieties of sounds that you have not heard before.

Exercise "The new sound of familiar things."

Do you pay attention to the sounds that accompany your usual activities - for example, cooking dinner, washing dishes, or reading a book? Listen again to these sounds - how water flows from a tap, with what sound a plate is placed on the table, how rusty pages are turned, etc. You may re-open the sounding world around you.

Exercise "Glasses"

Take two glasses, wine glasses, cups or plates. Lightly touch something with metal - a knife, spoon or fork - one of these items. Listen to the sound. Then tap the other and listen too. Is there any difference in the sounds? What is the difference? How would you articulate? A few more times, alternately touch one and the other object and compare the sound. Then touch something else, such as a wooden or plastic spatula, and compare the sound again. Experiment, changing the force of impact and the material of objects.

Exercise "Familiar voices."

Maybe it seems to you that you know the voices of loved ones well, but try to listen to them again. You may hear new notes and shades that were not paid attention to. Notice if there has been a change in the voices lately? What are these changes, what are they connected with, what can they talk about? How do the voices change depending on the mood, well-being of the owners, as well as on the topic of conversation? Set a goal to discover at least ten shades of the voices of your relatives and friends that you have not noticed before.

Exercises for reproducing sound images

Exercise "Sounds of the Day"

This exercise should be performed in the evening, but not before bedtime, and two or three hours before going to bed. Focus and remember everything that you have heard throughout the day, starting with the awakening and up to the present moment. Remember only sounds - voices, noises, all that remained in the memory. Imagine scrolling the soundtrack of a movie, and this movie is your date.

Check whether you remember the voices of the people you met. Can you play them in memory? Have you ever had moments when you stopped hearing what is happening? What is the reason, perhaps with fatigue or inattention? Try to scroll through the "soundtrack" in such places repeatedly - maybe you can still remember something?

Then try mentally scrolling the same "soundtrack" in the opposite direction - from the present moment to the moment of awakening. Strive to make the sounds in your imagination as clear as possible, as if you were hearing them.

Exercise "Favorite place."

Remember yourself in some place you love. Imagine you are there again. What did you hear around you? Mentally reproduce all the sounds that you can remember. Try to take them all at the same time. Remember sounds as much as possible, trying not to miss anything. If you do not remember any sounds, but you know that they were there, dummy them.

Exercise "Sounding world."

Listen to the sounds around you. Whatever you hear - try to mentally, from memory, reproduce this sound in your imagination. For example, a car drove outside. The sound is already verse, and you imagine that you heard it again. Repeat this with a few sounds you heard. If you have heard someone's conversation, immediately reproduce it in your memory, paying special attention to the sound of your voice, intonation, and speech rate.

Then turn on the radio or TV for just a few seconds and turn it off immediately. Mentally reproduce what you heard, again paying attention to the sound characteristics, and not just the meaning of the words (if it was a conversation).

This exercise can be performed at any time and in any place, mentally reproducing what you heard.

Exercise "Familiar voice."

Imagine that you hear someone's familiar voice — it says something. Imagine what you hear specifically - not so much the words, like timbre, tone, volume, emotional coloring. Imagine that the voice-first sounds somewhere far away, and then approaches you. How does the sound change? Imagine that your voice sounds quieter, louder, now lower, and then higher. You almost hear a whisper, but he goes on to scream, then speaks as usual. Then imagine how the pace of speech slows down and again accelerates, and now speaks very quickly, with a patter, but slowly again.

Then imagine how this voice sings something - at first quietly, and then louder, it sounds something higher, then lower. Nevertheless, you hear laughter. Then the voice says something in a joyful tone, and then it starts to sound sad.

Reproduce in your imagination a variety of modulations, trying to make as clear as possible the real sound of the voice.

Exercise "Combinations of Sounds"

Imagine any few sounds that come to mind - no less than five or seven. Let it be completely unrelated sounds. For example, the splashing of a wave, the crackling of a fire, the sound of a working drill, the sound of a computer keyboard, someone is singing. Your task is to connect them in your imagination so that you get some kind of holistic sound image. Consider, try to combine the sounds in different ways and as clearly as possible represent them, and each individually and collectively. It is important to be well aware of the sources of sound - no need to specifically create visual images, just imagine who sings and who types on a computer, or is it the same person? Who drills a drill, and how water and fire are connected with it. Once you present all the sounds, perhaps the image will be born by itself. It does not matter if it is not very realistic - it is important to get an experience of mentally combining sounds, linking together what seems to be unrelated.

Exercises on the mental creation of sound images
Exercise "Sound Pictures"
Focus and alternately draw the following sound patterns in your imagination:
• the sound of rain and wind
• the sound of a waterfall
• the sounds of the forest on a warm summer day
• seacoast
• river backwater
• mountain gorge
• city highway

- country house
- aircraft cabin
- quiet cafe
- hospitals
- factory floor
- libraries
- subway car

Exercise "New Home"

Imagine that you decided to settle in a new house. You have to choose a place to build it. Since sounds are important to you as an audience, you should choose a place where they will delight your ear. Decide for yourself what you would like to hear in your home. What sounds should be outside the window when you wake up? Mentally recreate them. What sounds should be in the house? Imagine them too. Try to recreate the whole range of sounds - sounds on the street, sounds in the room and behind the wall, etc. Make sure that you really like the overall sound. Try not to miss the little things - the clatter of dishes in the kitchen, the ticking of the clock, the noise of pouring water, opening doors, the creaking of floorboards, etc. In your imagination, pick up the sound that you really like.

Exercise "Transformation of sounds."

Imagine any sound you often hear - for example, a phone call or car noise outside the window. It is important that now this sound be only in your imagination - not in reality.

Your task is to mentally produce a series of transformations of this sound, changing its timbre, pitch, volume, presenting it closer, then further, etc. Important: change only the characteristics of the sound, but not its essence. That is, the phone call should remain a phone call, not turning into another sound in essence. However, you should try to repeatedly change its sound, changing, in turn, all the possible characteristics.

The more variations of sound you find, the better.

Exercise "Fantastic Sounds"

Imagine the same sound as in the previous exercise. Now your task is not just to modify it, but mentally turn it into something else. For example, imagine that your phone can speak in a human voice, and not because the voice is recorded in it, but because, for example, the phone is an animate being and is endowed with its own timbre. What kind of timbre do you think? Imagine it!

Then look at any items that you have in front of your eyes (or imagine any other items), and ask yourself a question about each of them: "How would his voice be if he could talk?"

How would a cup talk? What voice can a pencil or pen have? Moreover, if the chandelier could sing - in what voice would she do it?

Try to imagine and "hear" all these voices with your inner ear.

Exercise "Perfect Place"

Mentally transfer to any place that you like - absolutely real, where you have already been. Remember the sounds you heard there. Imagine that they have become more pleasant for you - melodious, louder, or, conversely, quieter. Let the most pleasant sounds sound more distinctly, and the sounds that you do not like, subside. And if you would like complete silence, imagine it.

Add some more sounds that were not in reality, but which you would like to hear. Enhance the sound picture of your favorite place so that it becomes almost perfect.

You can enjoy sounds or silence in the ideal place of your dreams, in which you can turn your favorite place.

Exercise "Old House"

Imagine that you were in an old house or even a palace, a castle. There is nobody besides you. Imagine opening doors and entering. What sounds is it accompanied by? What do you hear inside the house? Make any sounds that could get your attention. How would you react to these sounds? How would you behave when you hear them?

Imagine every sound of an old house - maybe it is a clock fight, the creaking of floorboards, the knock of a door opening, the wind slamming shutters. You can imagine that you have found a music box or some other sounding instrument. It all depends on your imagination. The more variety of sounds you imagine, the better.

Exercise "The sound of your name."

Imagine someone calling you by name. Whose voice is it? Where does the sound come from? Try to present it as clearly as possible.

Imagine that the sound is moving away and then approaching. Then it sounds to your right, then to your left, then above and below.

Listen, trying to determine where the sound is coming from, whether it is far or close.

Imagine that you are alternately hailed by the name of a female voice, then a male voice.

Imagine that they call you on a noisy city street.

Your name is called in the echoing silence of an empty university audience.

Someone says your name in a noisy stadium.

You hail into the train.

Someone called you during a film show in a dark cinema when there is a noisy scene on the screen.

Mentally reproduce the sound of all these imaginary voices, as if you were hearing them in reality.

Exercise "Concert"

Imagine that you are at a concert where the orchestra plays your favorite music. Mentally reproduce it in your imagination, as if you really sit at a concert and listen. Try to hear the whole orchestra as a whole and the sound of individual instruments.

Then imagine that a singer came on stage and sang your favorite song. Do not forget that the singer sings to the accompaniment of the orchestra; try to hear his voice and music at the same time.

Now imagine that you are the singer and sing a song on stage. Mentally sing it from beginning to end, imagining that you are accompanied by an orchestra.

Exercise "Different Voices"

Take any phrase, for example: "Life is beautiful!" Read it out loud, then silently. Then imagine that you can hear yourself from the side - as this phrase, pronounced by your voice, sounds.

Then imagine in turn who to say this phrase:

• your best friend

• someone from your family members

• child

• the very old man

• your favorite artist

• your favorite cartoon character

• your favorite literary hero

• robot

• alien

• talking dog

• clown in a circus

• TV announcer

• Barbie doll

• marathon runner on the run

• parachutist in free flight

• a freshwater diver who has just emerged

• a person falling asleep

- a   person   who   has   just   woken   up

If you want, you can try to reproduce out loud all these variations of the phrase. But the main thing is that you hear this sound as clearly as possible in your imagination.

Exercise "Musician"

Imagine that you are a musician who plays a musical instrument, anyone. You can imagine yourself at the piano; you can imagine that you have a guitar, a violin or a cello in your hands, etc. Imagine that you touch the strings or the keys and start extracting sounds. What kind of music is it? What is her pace, rhythm, what kind of melody are you playing? Try to hear all this with your inner ear as clearly as possible.

Remember that you are a musician, which means that you can change the sound of an instrument on your own, play it quieter or louder, faster or slower, change the tone, pitch, etc.

Imagine that you improvise, play, as you want. In your imagination, you can play both well-known works and music that you have not heard before - no matter how perfect your imaginary compositions will be. The main thing is to try to tune the inner ear to hear the music and control your imaginary playing on the instrument.

Exercise "Sound"

Take a reproduction of any picture that you like. Consider it and think about what sounds could be heard if this picture was, for example, a shot of the voiced movie. Imagine these sounds as clearly as possible. If this is a landscape - maybe there are birds singing, cicadas chirping, waves rustle or wind? If people are depicted - what are they talking about?

Even if it is a portrait or still life - the sounds are still present, because in reality there is no complete silence, even in silence there are sounds!

Having first presented realistic sounds, then complicate the task: imagine sounds that are completely inconsistent with the picture, or even contradict it. Imagine that you are a sound engineer, and you have the task to create a contrast between a picture and sounds. Such a technique is sometimes used in cinema to enhance the effect of the picture: for example, in the background of a peaceful landscape, one can hear someone speaking in raised voices.

Experiment, select different sounds for the picture, and you can get many unexpected effects, thus training your sound perception and the ability to recreate sounds in your imagination.

Exercise "Re-sound"

For this exercise, you will need a disc with your favorite movie (or video from the Internet). Turn off the sound and view a small excerpt from it. And if you remember well some excerpt from your favorite movie, then you can do without recording, just play it in memory. Now your task is to mentally re-sound this passage.

Imagine that the actors speak in completely different voices, different music sounds, and other sounds are heard. Go through different options; choose those that seem to you the most interesting. Experiment, selecting, it would seem, completely unsuitable sounds and voices. If you have the opportunity and desire, you can try and in reality to re-sound any excerpt of any film, recording a new soundtrack to it and then listen to what happened.

Exercise "Composer"

Listen carefully to the sound of the surrounding world. To focus better, you can close your eyes.

Imagine that you need to turn every sound you hear into a musical phrase. Try to hear the music in each sound - catch its rhythm, timbre, melody, and mentally make it sound musical.

For example, imagine:

• how the wind noise in the foliage sounded, if it were music;

• how the music transmits the sound of the surf, the singing of birds, the sound of a passing train;

• what kind of music would correspond to the sound of a typewriter, a computer keyboard, the sound of dishes, the noise of water flowing from a tap?

Try to mentally find a musical match even with such non-musical sounds, like:

• sounds of working construction,

• repair behind the wall,

• swearing neighbors.

Imagine how a whole piece of music on such topics could sound.

Exercises to help translate visual and kinesthetic information into sounds

Exercise "Picture and sound."

This exercise is intended for audials that have difficulty perceiving the world through other channels. An audial does not always catch the information coming through the visual channel, and even if it does, it is not sufficiently informative for it. But you can get much more information from visual images if you learn to "translate" them into your own "language," that is, into auditory images. To do this, you can use the association method - to represent the sound with which you associate certain visual images.

First, try to translate this or that color into sounds. It is no secret that sound vibrations have correspondences in the form of one or another color. If the color information is less close to you than the sound information, you can try to determine how the colors "sound."

Focus and try to imagine which sound corresponds to each color of the rainbow:

• red

• orange

• yellow

• green

• blue

• indigo

• violet

Perhaps some of these sounds are pleasant to you, and some are not? Through the perception of sound, you can better understand their color preferences.

Now let us complicate the task: determine how different forms are associated with sounds.

Try to mentally find a sound match to the following forms:
• oval
• triangle
• rectangle
• cone
• pyramid
• ball
• cube

Look for your own associations, without thinking about whether you answer "right" or "wrong." There are no right or wrong answers here because the perception of each person is individual. You need to find the answers that correspond to your perception.

Then you can go even further: determine what sounds correspond to different objects, things, phenomena of the world. Try to imagine, for example:
• how a wardrobe or a desk might sound;
• what is the timbre of the "voice" of a tree, flower, and grass;
• what note is associated with a soccer ball, tennis racket, basketball basket;
• how a crane, asphalt near the house, the house itself may sound.

Having identified sound associations, you will begin to understand better the information carried by the visuals.

Exercise "Sensation and sound."

This exercise is similar to the previous one; only now we will translate into sounds, not visual images, but sensations.

Determine what sound you associate with each of the following sensations:

• cold

• heat

• frost

• heaviness

• ease

• weightlessness

• the feeling of immersion in water

• breath of fresh air

• a touch of fine silk to the skin

• an apple that you hold in your hand

• touching the rough surface of granite

• dough, which you crush with hands

• touching cold metal

• prickly Christmas needles

Problem-solving exercises

Exercise "Voice problems"

For an audial, the solution of a problem begins precisely with the reconstruction of its sound image, as well as with sounding - that is, pronouncing out loud or at least a mental formulation of the essence of the problem. The audience needs to hear and formulate what the problem is - only then can it properly understand it, which means find the best solution. Often the problem is not solved by the audial precisely because it does not have a clear auditory understanding of it and of what needs to be done in order for the problem to be solved. The easiest way to understand the problem for an auditory is to perceive it in clear sound images.

Let us envision your troubles you would like to solve. For example, you would like to change jobs, but you have doubts, you are not sure that you know exactly what you want. Create for yourself a sound image of your current work. To do this, just remember everything you hear at work.

If this work really does not suit you, then the sounds will seem unpleasant to you. Determine where these sounds come from, what or who produces them. If you do not like the sounds, then do not like their sources. Therefore, you already come to the heart of the problem, realizing what specifically you would like to change.

Decide what you would like to hear instead of these sounds. For example, you would like it to be quieter or to make the sounds more pleasant, caressing the ear. Having determined exactly what you would like to hear in connection with work, you will be able to create for yourself a new, desired way of working, and it will help you make the right choice.

In the same way, you can deal with any problem: create its sound image, determine what exactly you do not like about it, and replace it with the desired images. Thanks to this, you can understand how to act in reality in order to arrive at the desired solution.

For the auditor, it is also important to formulate the problem, to voice it. Start by saying aloud what you do not like specifically - first the sounds you heard, then their sources. So say: "I don't like that at work I've heard all the time ..." So you will understand that first, you need to change to solve the problem.

Exercise "Sound solutions."

After completing the previous exercise, you determined what you do not like in the existing situation and what you would like to change. After this, it is not at all difficult to determine what you would like to receive in return. Replace what you do not like in the imagination with the exact opposite - what you might like.

For example, if you don't like noise at work, you'd like to work where it's quiet; if you don't like that it's too quiet at home, it would mean if the house was filled with the sound of dishes in the kitchen in the mornings, children's voices or, for example, music.

Having realized what you would like, you can create a sound image of the solved problem. Even if you do not know yet how to approach the solution to a problem, you can imagine that the problem has already been solved. Imagine yourself in a situation where the problem is solved, and imagine all that you will hear around yourself in a given situation (for example, in a new job, in a new house, etc.). Let the sound image be as detailed as possible, clear, and distinct.

Important: imagine the combination of sounds that you like.

As a result, you will know exactly what you want. Your brain will get the task to solve the problem in the best way for you. Your intellectual and creative abilities will awaken, and it will be easier for you to begin to act in the right direction.

Exercise "Getting rid of unwanted experiences."

Thanks to your sensitivity to sounds, you can learn to cope with a bad mood, get rid of negative experiences, and even throw off the burden of problems stretching from the past.

Think about some situation that upset you, or unpleasant memories, from the influence of which I would like to get rid of. Remember the sounds that accompanied this event. It can be someone's voices, your own voice, and all other sounds that you remember.

First, imagine that all these sounds are very loud and you hear them very close to you.

Then imagine that the sounds become quieter as if their sources are moving away from you. Now they are barely audible, the sound from afar. For example, if someone scolded you and it stuck in your memory, imagine that the person who scolded you is very far away so that his voice barely reaches you. You no longer understand the words; you hear only individual sounds and intonations. Nevertheless, here they are subsiding. You no longer hear annoying sounds.

Notice how your feelings have changed with it. When you mentally distance yourself and force all sounds accompanying negative experiences to subside, the experiences themselves will disappear; negative emotions will no longer have power over you.

If you cannot immediately make the sounds associated with an unpleasant situation subside, first try to change their sound characteristics: for example, speed up, or, on the contrary, slow down the speech of the one who scolds you, then make him speak in a very high or very low voice, then let he will speak in the voice of Pinocchio, or some kind of cartoon character. Such transformations will instantly reduce the degree of influence of this voice on you. After that, it will be easier to mentally distance him from yourself and imagine that you no longer hear him.

Successful Exercises

Exercise "Positive attitude"

Using sound images, you can at any time create a positive attitude for yourself, get a surge of strength and energy, tune in to work, creativity, success, a state of joy and happiness. To do this, you only need to remember when you have already been in such a state - and mentally reproduce sounds corresponding to this situation.

For example, you would like to be in a state where you felt strong and confident. Close your eyes and remember the situation when you felt like that.

Remember what you heard then. If possible, reproduce all sounds in your imagination. Remember how the voices sounded. Whose were these voices? What exactly did they say? Remember if someone laughed, or maybe it was your laugh. Remember how other emotions were expressed in the sound.

Then imagine that all these sounds have become even louder, more distinct and that they have added positive emotions. For example, laughter becomes applause that is even more joyful, louder; someone's kind words to you are more enthusiastic and solemn, and so on.

Mentally bring these sounds closer to you, as if they are right next to you, sound right in your ears.

You will notice that a pleasant state of confidence and strength will not only arise among you by itself but will even become even more distinct than before. This was because you enhanced the positive sound signals, which, entering into your brain, allowed it to activate a state of confidence and strength.

In the same way, you can reinforce any positive state — by amplifying the accompanying sound information.

Exercise "Image of Success"

This exercise will help you to instantly enter a state of success if you determine for yourself exactly which sound characteristics of your image correspond to success. You can remember yourself when you managed everything, and you felt successful. How did your voice sound? Surely, he was more sonorous, loud, and confident than when you doubted something or made mistakes. But the most important thing is the thoughts that were in your head in the form of a word. The audience is a very important language. Even if they are not spoken aloud, he still perceives them precisely through hearing - imagining how they would sound.

First, imagine yourself as you speak loudly, confidently, convincingly, in a loud, beautiful voice, expressive, rich in modulations and a variety of intonations. Even if in reality, you do not have such a voice, creating a similar mental image, you will soon begin to really come close to such an ideal sound.

Then formulate for yourself the thoughts that accompany the state of success, for example: "Everything works out for me," "Everything is fine," "I am confident in myself," "I believe in my success." Imagine yourself speaking these phrases in the most confident, beautiful, and sonorous voice. Subsequently, you can begin to say aloud these phrases exactly as you imagined.

If you present yourself with the voice and thoughts associated with success, your brain will receive a command and in reality, start working on such your transformation.

Exercise "How the dream sounds."

This exercise will help you achieve your goals, tuning you to the perception of sounds accompanying them.

Close your eyes and imagine that the dream came true. It is very important to imagine everything that you will hear in this situation. Sounds should be pleasant to you. If the sounds are pleasant, your brain will guide you along the path to achieving the goal. If there is anything unpleasant in sounds, remove this unpleasant image, and replace it with another, pleasant one.

Try not to miss anything that you would like to hear when your goal is reached. Decide what exactly it should be - if there are human voices, what and what they say if the music is what and where exactly it comes from if the sounds of nature are what they sound like.

Having created the fullest possible sound picture of a dream come true; imagine that you are inside this picture. Listen to the sounds as if they surround you. Then make them even more pleasant, sonorous. If you want, you can mentally turn it down or turn up the volume, depending on how you like. Create for yourself the perfect sound of your dream come true. At this point, you are bringing yourself closer to your cherished goal, even if you have not yet taken any real steps to achieve it.

Chapter 7. Exercises for kinesthetics

E xercise "What I feel now"
A kinesthetic get much more information from sensations than from visual images and sounds. It is not so important for him that he sees and hears – but how he feels. In any case, many people are inattentive to their feelings. And if it's not so scary for a visual and an audial, then for kinesthetics it's a real disaster. Without tracking your feelings, you can misinterpret important information. The simplest example: without noticing that the shoes chosen in the store are uncomfortable, you can throw a considerable amount of money down the drain by buying shoes that you cannot wear.

Therefore, attention to sensations must be trained, and this is especially important for kinesthetics because for them this is the main channel for perceiving information from the outside world, that is, the information coming through this channel is the most accurate for them.

Close your eyes, concentrate, and ask yourself the question: "What am I feeling right now?" Focus on the sensations in your body. Be careful and enumerate everything that you notice: warm or cool, whether there is tension or heaviness in some parts of the body, how clothes touch the skin, you are sitting on something soft or hard, whether you feel awake or sluggish, if something hurts, if your heart is pounding too much, how you breathe, are you full, or have a feeling of hunger, thirst, etc.

You will notice that the body gives you a lot of signals in the form of sensations, some of them are pleasant, some are not very or even completely uncomfortable. In addition, not all these signals are random. They confirm either that you are doing well and correctly, or are pushing for change, warning you that you should pay special attention to your condition. It is impossible to dismiss these signals; you need to listen to them. In addition, think: what needs to be done so that the uncomfortable sensations change to comfortable ones. Sometimes the solution is simple: for example, if it is cold, just dress warmly. Sometimes it is not very simple: for example, if the heart is pounding strongly, it means that you are agitated and, perhaps, you need to take some decision and perform some action to eliminate the cause of this excitement.

Nevertheless, this is the next step, and the first is attention to sensations. Try to pay more attention to your condition and answer the question: "What am I feeling now?"

Exercise "Touch the familiar"

There are many familiar things around you - those that you see and deal with every day. These are dishes - cups, plates, spoons, and appliances - telephones, laptops and computer mice, TV remote controls and radios, and clothing, personal items - bags, gloves, hats, etc. Do you remember what all these are? Things to the touch, or do not pay attention to tactile sensations?

Take in your hands anything you often use, close your eyes, and feel it well. Be attentive to your feelings. Call what you feel specifically - the surface is smooth or rough, soft or hard, how the material and the shape of the thing are perceived by touch. Notice the details, all sorts of bends, bumps, depressions, rounding, etc. Study the subject for at least one minute, and you will have the feeling that you have met it again.

Exercise "Apples"

Take two apples and examine them alternately with your eyes closed with the help of touch. Try to find as many differences as possible that can be identified by touch. Compare the size and shape, the sensations of touching the skin, cutting, surface irregularities, etc. Then open your eyes and check if you could see with your eyes the differences that you found to your touch. Usually, kinesthetic can learn much more about an object with the help of touch than with the help of their eyes.

Exercise "Sensations in the muscles."

Lightly circular movements, massage yourself first one hand, then the other. Focus on the sensations. When you finish massaging, again "listen" to the sensations: you will notice that in your hands there is still a feeling of touch, kneading of muscles. Massage your neck and upper back, as far as you can get.

Close your eyes and again focus on the sensations that remained after the massage. You will feel the muscles relax as if the massage is going on. Note whether these sensations are pleasing to you. If you want, you can ask someone from your loved ones to massage you and again focus on the sensations.

Then move around a bit, squat, or make a few bends, or just go for a walk on the spot. Attention to sensations in the muscles! Try to understand what movements your body is asking for and make those movements that leave a pleasant feeling behind you.

83

Develop the habit of listening to your body - which position is more pleasant for him to take, and which poses, on the contrary, seem to be inconvenient; which activities give pleasure, what kind of physical activity suits you. A body that is taken care of is capable of giving in the form of sensations more accurate and complete information about the world around it.

Exercises on the development of the ability to mentally reproduce kinesthetic images

Exercise "Feelings of this day."

This exercise should be performed in the evening, but not before bedtime, and two or three hours before going to bed. Focus and remember everything that you felt, felt, felt during the day, starting with awakening and up to the present moment. Remember only the sensations - for example, how did you feel when you were taking a shower, brushing your teeth, having breakfast, getting dressed, going to work and so on up to the present moment. Was it convenient for you? Was there any discomfort due to uncomfortable clothing, heat or cold, or, for example, a crowded subway train? What feelings did you have with different people you had to communicate with? If you touched someone (for example, shaking hands), what was that touch? Remember it and mentally reproduce it.

Did you feel the floor on which you walk, the chair on which you sit, did you remember the sensations from the objects you took in your hands? Were there moments when you suddenly seemed to lose sensitivity? What is the reason - perhaps with fatigue, tension, or preoccupation with your thoughts? Try to scroll through the memory of these moments again and still remember what exactly you felt then.

Then try mentally scrolling all the sensations of the day in the opposite direction - from the present moment to the moment of awakening. Strive to make sensations perceived in your imagination as clearly as possible, as if you were experiencing them again.

Exercise "Favorite place."

Remember yourself in someplace you love. Imagine you are there again. What did you feel? Imagine again that you feel the same. You will notice that the body has a memory and it easily reproduces the sensation of a light breeze, and a soft enveloping touch of warm seawater, and the barb of grass under bare feet, and the fragrance of flowers, and the warmth of the sun's rays. Try to remember as many sensations as possible related to your favorite place and perceive them all at the same time. You will have the feeling that you are transported back to where you like it so much.

Exercise "Memory of touches."

Take any small object — for example, a coin, a pen, a pebble — and attach it to your hand. Several times, change the position of the object, putting it to different areas, first one hand, and then the other. Focus on sensations and try to memorize them. Then set the subject aside. Continue to hold the touch of the subject to the skin mentally. Then imagine that you are applying it again first to one hand, then to the other. Reproduce the sensations of touch.

Then imagine that you are applying this object to other parts of the body, for example to the leg, to the neck. You will notice that it is easy to reproduce the feeling of touching the skin, although you touch an imaginary rather than a real object.

The exercise "Memory movements."

Make some movement — for example, bend the arm at the elbow and straighten it. Remember the sensations. Now do the same in imagination, reproducing all sensations associated with movement.

Perform a few more movements, for example, from the morning gymnastics. Memorize the sensations. Then lie down or sit in a relaxed position and imagine that you are performing these movements. Watch for sensations in the body.

Now, without leaving a free, relaxed posture, remember the movements that you are well acquainted with: for example, imagine that you are taking a quick step along the street; swim in the pool; riding a bicycle; you are skating or skiing, etc. Try to reproduce in your body all the sensations associated with these movements, as if you really are doing something similar now.

Exercise "familiar feelings."

Every person has experience with many sensations. If you want, you can remember them and even feel as if you feel it again. Remember and imagine:

• touching something prickly
• a touch of something soft

- touching the rough surface
- feeling like you are carrying something heavy
- feeling like you are throwing the ball
- feeling like you are running
- touching the ice
- touch of the foot to the hot sand or stones on the beach
- feeling when you wash your hands with cold water
- drink hot tea
- turn over the book page
- write something with a pen on paper
- inhale fresh cool air
- wear a wool hat
- swim
- relaxing under a soft blanket

Exercises to create imaginary kinesthetic images

Exercise "Untested Feelings"

This is an exercise of imagination, which invites you to experience those imaginary sensations that you did not experience in reality. For example, you never jumped with a parachute. Imagine you do it. Here you step into the abyss, experience free fall, so the parachute opens, and you soar gently and smoothly in space, look down at the landscape below and finally touch the earth safely.

You can imagine yourself as a deep-sea diver, a climber, an airplane pilot, an astronaut, anyone else, to understand what feelings a person experiences in such situations.

Exercise "Museum"

Imagine that you went to a museum, where there are many interesting exhibits that you cannot touch (or actually go there - for example, to a local history museum). You can also use the illustrations, which depict such museum exhibits. Carefully examining each of them, imagine that you touch them, explore with the help of touch. Try to imagine as clearly as possible how your hands feel when they touch you.

Exercise "Actor"

Remember some of your favorite movies. Imagine that you are an actor playing the main role. You should not only act in this image but also feel what the performer and his hero feel. Mentally live with him a small excerpt from the film, perceiving what is happening no longer as a spectator, not from the outside, but in the way that the hero perceives it. If he is cold, imagine how you feel cold; if he is in motion, mentally move like him, and so on.

Exercise "Literary hero."

Re-read any passage from a book, where your favorite literary hero acts. Put yourself in his place and try to understand what he feels. Even if the author does not describe the actual sensations, you can speculate because of the circumstances in which the character falls, from the description of what surrounds him. Even if nothing like this has ever happened to you, you can dream up and imagine what feelings you would have felt if you were in the place of this hero.

Exercise "New interior."

Imagine that you decided to change the interior in your house completely - to update the furniture, finish, maybe, to do redevelopment. Since sensations are important to you as kinesthetic, decide for yourself what you would like to feel in your renovated home. Imagine a bed that is comfortable for you, such an arrangement of furniture that everything is at hand, such fabrics and finishing materials that you will be pleased to touch, etc.

Try not to forget any trifles and details and mentally design your home so that you would like all the sensations experienced there. Then imagine that you are already in this new interior - you live there, sleep, move, do different things, take a shower, prepare food, and all this with a whole range of pleasant sensations. You can even mentally live the whole day in such an ideal interior, presenting all these sensations as a reality.

Exercise "Transformation sensations."

Imagine any feeling familiar to you — for example, a feeling of light coolness. Recall it and realize that you are experiencing it again. Your task is to gradually move from this feeling to its opposite; in our case, it is warm. But you need not just to imagine the heat after the coolness, but to somehow justify this transition, for example, to imagine that you are wearing a warm sweater or come to a kindled stove. Do all this in your imagination, first imagining that you are cool, then imagining that you decided to wear a sweater, that you put it on (feel this process too), and now you gradually get warm, it becomes warmer and warmer.

Choose a few more sensations and in the same way modify them in your imagination, for example, imagine that you came out of the water, your body is wet - but here you wipe or gradually dry out in the sun; you carry a heavy backpack and gradually release it, and it becomes easy for you, and so on.

Exercise "Perfect Place"

Mentally transfer to any place that you like - absolutely real, where you have already been. Remember the sensations that you experienced there. If you like the place, it was a pleasant feeling. Imagine that they became even more pleasant. For example, the sea is even warmer and tenderer; the fragrance of flowers is even thinner, the air is still cleaner, the sand under your feet is even softer, etc. If there, you experienced any discomfort, imagine that it disappeared and was replaced by something pleasant.

Add some more sensations that were not in reality, but which you would like to experience, being in a comfortable place for you. You can imagine that you move as you like, eat and drink something tasty, inhale the most desirable aromas, lie on something soft, like a swan's down, or even feel light and weightless as if you have no weight and you are just floating in space. In this way, you will create in your imagination the ideal feelings that you only dream of. Moreover, despite the fact that such a place exists only in your dream, you can quite really enjoy the most pleasant sensations, mentally transferring there.

Exercise "Old House"

Imagine that you were in an old house or even a palace, a castle. There is nobody besides you. Imagine opening doors and entering. What do you feel about it? Is it cool or warm? What smells? What do your legs feel when stepping on the floor? In addition, hands, touching the doors, switches, objects.

Imagine yourself walking around the house and finding there many amazing things that you want to touch. Maybe you open a casket or an old chest. Imagine what is inside there, and imagine that you pick up everything, feel its weight, shape, surface. You sort out; feel things - figurines, dishes, maybe items of clothing. It all depends on your imagination. The more diverse sensations you imagine - and imagine that you are experiencing them - the better.

Exercise "Dark Room"

Imagine that you are in a room where it is completely dark. You can only move around by touch. You find that the room is rather cramped; there are many things in it. Every now and then, you come across them. What do you feel? Can you tell by your feelings what these things are? Some subjects you are especially interested, and you feel them. Imagine all the sensations that you would have experienced.

Exercise "Manicure"

Imagine that you are doing a manicure. First, you immerse your hands in a bath of warm water. Imagine the pleasant warmth of the water, warming your hands, bubbles on the surface of the water, the smell of aromatic oil added to the water. Then you take a soft, fluffy towel and carefully wipe each finger. With the help of special tools you clean, erode, polish your nails. Imagine the touch of each tool: spatulas, nail files, scissors, and tweezers. Then you cover the nails with a foundation for nail polish. Imagine its sharp smell. When drying, the base cools the nails slightly, but you like it. Now take a varnish and carefully paint every nail. Try to do this carefully, barely touching the surface of the nail with a brush. Feel the smell of varnish, which disappears as soon as the nails dry. Finally, imagine the result: beautifully painted nails of perfect shape. Swipe your finger across the surface of the nail, feel how smooth it is.

Exercise "Combinations of feelings."

What are some sensations, no less than five or seven, that will come to your mind first, for example, warmth, heaviness, the taste of coffee, touching a rough stone, soft fabric? First, imagine that you experience each of these sensations in turn. Then imagine trying them all at once. It does not matter if the set turns out to be incompatible at first glance - this will complicate the task, but make it more interesting! Combining all these sensations, try to imagine a situation in which you could experience it all at once. Imagine yourself in this situation, adding more sensations that you think you could experience in it.

Exercise "handshakes."

Remember a simple gesture - a handshake. Remember some familiar handshakes and imagine that you feel them again.

Then alternately imagine that you are shaking hands with:

• a young, strong, healthy man

• a tender girl

• a small child

• your favorite movie character

• an old, weak person

• a person who shakes hands with you according to the official protocol

• a person who is sincerely glad to meet you

It is possible to represent different handshakes not in a row, but with breaks. The main thing is that you feel as clearly as possible how each of them is felt.

Exercise "If I Was a Tree"

How do you think the tree feels? We certainly cannot know this, but in imagination everything is possible! Imagine yourself a tree - powerful, strong, and firmly rooted in the ground. Imagine how it absorbs water and nutrients from the earth, and vital sap rises up the trunk. Imagine how the buds burst. Imagine how the wind makes the leaves tremble, how they are washed by the rain, warmed by the sun. Try to experience all these sensations in your imagination.

You can complicate the exercise by imagining yourself as an inanimate object. What does the chair feel when you sit on it? Paper, when do you write on it? The window when you open it and wash? Do not let slip from memory; ;this is just for fun. Do not seriously try to become a window or table - play it. Nevertheless, your feelings, though born of the imagination, will be quite real.

Exercises to help translate visual images and sounds into sensations

Exercise "Picture and feeling."

This exercise is intended for kinesthetics, who have difficulties with the perception of the world through other channels. A kinesthetic does not always catch the information coming through the visual channel, and even if he does, it is not sufficiently meaningful for him. But you can get much more information from visual images if you learn to "translate" them into your own "language," that is, into kinesthetic images, into sensations. To do this, you can use the method of associations - to represent the feeling with which you associate certain visual images.

First, try to translate this or that color into sensations. It is no secret that there are colors warm and cold. Note also that one color may seem soft, and the other hand, one smooth, the other rough, and so on.

Focus and try to imagine what sensations correspond to each color of the rainbow:

• red

• orange

• yellow

• green

• blue

• indigo

• violet

With each color, you may not even be associated with one feeling, but several. Do not look for "right" or "wrong" associations - they should be your own because each person can have an individual perception of color.

Perhaps some of these sensations are pleasant to you, and some are not? Through the perception of sensations, you can better understand color preferences.

Now let us complicate the task: determine how different forms are associated with sensations. Try to find sensations corresponding to the following forms mentally:

• oval

• triangle

• rectangle

• cone

• pyramid

• ball

• cube

It's not that hard, is it? An oval is something smooth; a triangle is sharp, and so on. Let's further complicate the task: imagine which of these figures are associated with heat, and which with cold, and from what material, do you think they are made. Maybe from ice, iron, plastic, soft felt, etc.? Again, do not think about the "correctness" or "incorrectness" of the answers - look for your own, individual, subjective associations.

Then you can go even further: to determine which feelings give rise to exactly different objects, things, phenomena of the world around you. You need to tune in to yourself, be attentive to your feelings, and then you can understand:

• what do you feel standing next to a skyscraper

• what sensations does the sight of a fast passing train make you

• what are your feelings when you see a kitten or other pet

• what do you feel when you see something beautiful, for example, a work of art

• what associations and sensations do the kind of freshly laid asphalt cause you, etc.

Determine whether these associations are pleasant or unpleasant, whether the sensations caused by these or those objects are comfortable. Having identified these kinesthetic associations, you will begin to understand better the information carried by the visuals. For example, the appearance of something very beautiful will not deceive you anymore if you realize that you are experiencing discomfort when you see it. This will save you from unnecessary shopping, and from visiting places you do not need, and from meeting with people from whom you can expect trouble.

Exercise "Sound and Sensation"
This exercise is similar to the previous one, only now we will translate into sensations, not visual images, but sounds.

Some sounds, like colors, may seem warm, and some – cold. Some are frost on the skin, and some - like a touch of a gentle sea wave, some sounds are rough, and some are smooth...

Determine how you are associated with each of the following sounds:

- thunder Strike
- ambulance siren
- knocking a heavy object on the floor
- the sound of an airplane taking off
- nightingale trill
- cock cry
- knocking typewriter
- the rustle of the wind in the branches
- the sound of the sea surf
- meowing cats
- bell ringing

Problem-solving exercises
Exercise "Feel the problem."

For kinesthetics, the solution of a problem begins with its perception in the language of sensations. Kinesthetics need to feel what the problem is - only then can it properly understand it, which means find the best solution. The easiest way to understand the problem for a kinesthetic is to perceive it in understandable kinesthetic images.

Think about the problem or problems you would like to solve. For example, you would like to change jobs, but you have doubts, you are not sure that you know exactly what you want. Focus on how you feel at work and in connection with it.

If this work really does not suit you, then these feelings are unpleasant. Determine what exactly caused the discomfort or in connection with which they arise. Thanks to this, you can move from a generalized judgment "Do not like work" to a concrete idea of what exactly you do not like about work. If, for example, you don't like the feeling in your fingers, the muscles of your hands, on your skin, when you hold any work tool, it means that this particular profession does not suit you, but if these feelings are pleasant, then the appearance of colleagues causes an unpleasant feeling of chills on the skin - it means that you need to think about another team where you could do the same. So you get to the heart of the problem, knowing exactly what you would like to change.

Then you can determine what feeling you would like to experience at work instead of these unpleasant ones. Therefore, you can create for yourself a new, desired image of work, and it will help you make the right choice.

In the same way, you can deal with any problem: be aware of the sensations that you experience in connection with it, determine what exactly you do not like about them, and replace them with the desired sensations. Thanks to this, you can understand how to act in reality in order to arrive at the desired solution.

Exercise "Feel the Solution"

After completing the previous exercise, you determined what you do not like in the current situation and what you would like to change. After this, it is not at all difficult to determine what you would like to receive in return. Replace what you don't like in the imagination with the exact opposite - what you might like. For example, if you don't like the cold at work, then you'd like to work where it is warm; I don't like that it's stuffy and crowded at home, so I'd like it if the house was filled with fresh air (most likely it's a country house), it was spacious.

Having realized what you would like, you can create a kinesthetic image of the solved problem. Even if you do not know yet how to approach the solution to a problem, you can imagine that the problem has already been solved. Imagine yourself in a situation where the problem is solved, and imagine all that you will feel in this situation (for example, in a new job, in a new house, etc.). Let the kinesthetic image be as detailed as possible, clear, and distinct.

Important: imagine exactly the combination of sensations that you like. As a result, you will know exactly what you want. Your brain will get the task to solve the problem in the best way for you. Your intellectual and creative abilities will awaken, and it will be easier for you to begin to act in the right direction.

Exercise "Getting rid of unwanted experiences."

Thanks to your sensitivity to feelings, you can learn to cope with a bad mood, get rid of negative experiences, and even throw off the burden of problems stretching from the past.

Think about some situation that upset you, or unpleasant memories, from the influence of which you would like to get rid of. Remember the sensations that accompanied this event. Consider their whole spectrum: whether you felt cold or warm, tension or lethargy, what were the smells around, how you felt what you were wearing, what you were standing or sitting on, what other people were feeling about you.

First, imagine that you are experiencing all these sensations again right now and they are very strong.

Then imagine that the discomfort gradually subsides. Now you almost do not feel them. Finally, they disappear completely, and opposing; pleasant sensations begin to take their place. For example, if a chill hit you, and then pleasant warmth envelops you if you are tense, then relax and calm down. If something hurts, the pain goes away.

Notice how your mood has changed with it. If you are the owner of your feelings, if you can change them at will, then you are the owner of your condition, mood, and therefore your life. It is in your power to eliminate unpleasant experiences and replace them with pleasant ones. Having got rid of unpleasant sensations, you will get rid of the negative emotions that the experience from the past carried.

Successful Exercises

Exercise "Positive attitude"

Using kinesthetic images, you can at any time create for yourself a positive attitude, get a surge of strength and energy, tune in to work, creativity, success, a state of joy and happiness. To do this, you just need to remember when you have already been in such a state - and mentally reproduce the sensations corresponding to this situation.

For example, you would like to be in a state where you felt strong and confident.

Close your eyes and remember the situation when you felt like that.

Remember all your feelings to the smallest detail, including smells, the taste of food. In addition, of course, remember what your body felt. For example, remember cheerfulness, strength, as you were in a pleasant tone, you felt light and mobile; all movements were precise and elegant. Remember your inner state with it and mentally reproduce these sensations, as if you are feeling all this again.

Then imagine that all these sensations have become even more pleasant and stronger, more distinct. Strengthen them as much as possible.

You will notice that a pleasant state of confidence and strength will not only arise among you by itself but will even become even more distinct than it was in reality. This is because you have enhanced the positive kinesthetic signals that, entering into your brain, allowed it to activate a state of confidence and strength.

In the same way, you can reinforce any positive state - enhancing the sensations that accompany it.

Exercise "Image of Success"

This exercise will help you instantly enter a state of success if you determine for yourself exactly which kinesthetic characteristics of your image correspond to success. You can remember yourself when you managed everything, and you felt successful. How did you feel? How did you move, what was your posture, what was your sense of self? It is also important to remember those objects that you touched, and smells, and the air temperature where you were.

Imagine that you are again in that setting and feel it all. If you again experience all the sensations associated with success, your brain will receive a command and in reality, lead you from success to success.

Exercise "Feel the dream."

This exercise will help you achieve your goals, setting you up to the perception of their attendant sensations.

Close your eyes and imagine that your cherished dream has come true. It is very important to imagine all that you will feel in this situation. Feelings should be pleasant for you. If the sensations are pleasant, your brain will guide you along the path to achieving the goal. If there is at least something unpleasant in the sensations, mentally eliminate this unpleasant aspect and replace it with another, pleasant one.

Try not to miss anything that you would like to feel when your goal is achieved. Having created the fullest possible kinesthetic image of a realized dream, imagine that you are inside this image. You feel it all right now!

Make the sensations even more pleasant and increase their intensity. Recreate all those feelings that seem to you the best, ideal, fully consistent with your idea of the dream realized. At this point, you are bringing yourself closer to your cherished goal, even if you have not yet taken any real steps to achieve it.

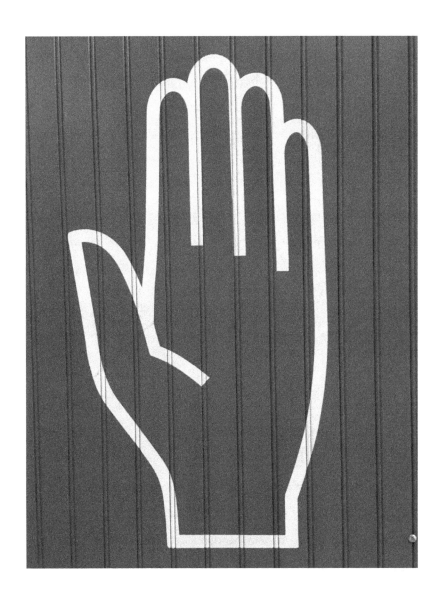

Chapter 8. Recommendations for visuals, audials, and kinesthetics

Each person is talented in something, endowed with abilities; each has a large unclaimed intellectual potential. But each of these abilities and capabilities - their own, unique, not similar to others. Everyone is talented and clever in his own way; this must be taken into account both in teaching, and in choosing a profession, in solving any life tasks, and in shaping the way of life that is right for you.

Visuals, audials, and kinesthetics not only perceive the world differently - they assimilate information differently and therefore react differently to the surrounding reality. In addition, how we react depends on how we act. If you want to act more efficiently, make the right decisions, it is better to assimilate knowledge, to memorize information, and understand what is happening around - consider your individual characteristics!

You will become much more successful in everything, whatever you undertake if you start practicing the techniques and methods of intellectual activity suitable for your type of perception.

This will help you not only in work and school but also in your daily life. After all, we need the work of the intellect at every step - whether we are shopping, building routes around the city, doing household work, or planning a vacation. Think about what problems you are most likely to pursue in such daily affairs. If you lack self-organization, if you are often late, forget what you have to do, confuse names, spend too much time on simple things, etc., then you need to reconsider the approach to this kind of tasks. If this approach matches your type of perception, your life will become easier, and its quality will increase markedly

Further, you will read specific practical tips for visuals, audials, and kinesthetics. Start using them in your daily life right from today and compare the results with those that you had before.

Tips for visuals

1. Make plans for yourself every day in writing - briefly on a piece of paper indicate all the things that need to be done in a day. Highlight the most important ones with a bright marker or underline or write with a felt-tip pen of a different color. As you complete the tasks, put a tick next to the relevant item of the plan or cross out this item.

2. Keep a diary - record the dates and times of important meetings and events. This does not mean that you should not rely on your memory. But having written down, you easier remember the necessary information.

3. Going to the grocery store, not only make a list if necessary but also imagine all that is to be bought.

4. If you need to learn something new, give preference to sources (magazines, newspapers, prospectuses, books, Internet resources), where there are many illustrations. The information content of the text provided with illustrations for you will increase many times over the same, but not illustrated text.

5. If it is important for you to learn and remember well what another person is saying, look into his face. If you have an important conversation, give preference to a personal meeting, rather than a

telephone conversation. If it is not possible to meet in person, then during a telephone conversation, make brief notes with a pen on paper, writing down the main content of the conversation.

6. If you are given a task - for example, for work - immediately write it down, and then lay it down in writing on the items and main stages of implementation.

7. If you need to remember well some information, imagine it in the form of images, visible pictures as if watching an imaginary film.

8. If you have some important event ahead - exam, performance, meeting, interview, negotiation - in advance rehearse in front of the mirror what you will say and how to behave. In addition, even better - shoot yourself on a video camera. After viewing the recording and seeing yourself from the outside, you can feel much more confident during a responsible event.

9. Try to rest and recuperate in places previously unfamiliar to you, where there is a lot of new and diverse "food for the eyes": beautiful landscapes, architectural monuments, etc.

10. Design your home and workplace so that the interior is pleasing to the eye.

Tips for audials

1. Every morning, say out loud all that you have to do. If you are afraid to forget, record it on your recorder and keep it with you so that you can listen to the recording at any time.

2. As a reminder, use a variety of audible signals - alarm calls, timer signals, etc.

3. When you go shopping, first make a list and then speak it out loud.

4. If you need to learn something new, try to get information from audio sources - these can be audiobooks, lecture notes, webinars, etc. Visit the live lectures more often; use the opportunities to get oral advice from a specialist, to attend a seminar, etc.

5. If you have an important conversation, try not to be distracted by the appearance of the interlocutor, fully focus on the meaning of his words. To do this, from time to time, take your eyes off his face, turning your head slightly to the side as if you would like to hear better what he says. At the same time, with slight nods of your head, witnessing and your attentive look, demonstrate your interest (so that the interlocutor does not think that you are not listening, just turned away). If possible, use a voice recorder to record the words of the interlocutor, and then listen to them again in a relaxed atmosphere. In many cases, important conversations are preferable to you on the phone (when it is more important to hear than to see the interlocutor).

6. When you are given some task for work, immediately repeat aloud what you have to do, ask questions, if something is not clear, ask for detailed verbal explanations.

7. If you need to remember some information, immediately speak it aloud.

8. If you are to take an exam or another important event, rehearse aloud everything you say. Better yet, record yourself on the recorder and listen to it.

9. Rest and recuperation are better for you in silence. Periodic listening to quiet, calm music, sounds of nature will also be beneficial.

10. Equipping your home and workplace, make sure that there is quiet. If you need to spend money on sound insulation - for you it is an absolute must. Do not turn on the TV and other audio sources at full volume. If noise from neighboring rooms or from the street interferes, use earplugs, especially for sleeping.

Tips for kinesthetics

1. Making a plan for the day, pre-imagine what you will feel in a given situation, doing this or that action. This will help you better prepare and more successfully cope with any tasks.

2. To remind yourself of upcoming events, it is better to use some objects that you can hold in your hands, feeling their texture. For example, write important tasks on different cards, cards with different drawings, different density, and size.

3. Going to the grocery store, make a list, and imagine the taste of each product. If it is not products, then present the invoice of these goods, what they feel.

4. New information you best learn in practice. Prefer practical seminars, video tutorials, systematic instructions, and other sources were not only

theoretical but also practical material is given. It is necessary to say that kinesthetics is essentially a practice; therefore, activities that do not have a quick practical application (for example, theoretical science) are not interesting for them. This must be considered when choosing a profession and place of work.

5. If you have an important conversation, try to feel the energy or aura of the interlocutor (kinesthetics do it like no one else), tune in with it on a common wave, create a unified atmosphere of communication. Listening to what he says, pass information through your feelings. Listen to the inner feelings that evoke his words, listen to your intuition.

6. If you are given a job assignment, ask immediately to show in practice how this is done, or an example of a similar task already completed by others.

7. If you need to remember some information, associate what you need to remember with specific feelings and sensations. For example, you read about some historical episode - imagine not so many visual images as the general atmosphere. Envision cold or heat, smells and all that, as it seems to you, its participants felt.

8. If you are to take an exam or other important events, you should prepare for it best of all, sitting in a comfortable position, in a state of relaxation and always in privacy. For better memorization of information, you can repeat it on the go, for example, walking around the room or combining it with any other kind of movement that you like.

9. You need to rest and recuperate in a comfortable and pleasant environment, where you can relax and where you can experience various pleasant sensations - for example, undergo a course of the massage, aromatherapy, and spa treatments or just swim, take a walk, get some fresh air.

10. Equipping your home and workplace, make sure that your body is comfortable. Furniture must be comfortable. All that you touch should cause only pleasant tactile sensations. You also need a place to rest (for example, a chair where you can change from behind the desktop) and the ability to move (at least walk around the office, thinking about important ideas).

Tips to help communicate

In order to fully communicate with other people, it is simply necessary to understand not only your type of perception but also other people's ways of understanding the world. If we take into account who is in front of us - visual, audial or kinesthetic, then we will avoid many mistakes that occur when people speak as if in different languages without hearing or understanding each other.

For example, a mother makes a remark to a teenage son: "Can you not see that there is a mess in the room!" She is a visual and does not take into account that the kinesthetic son can really *not see* this disorder, or rather, see, but not notice, because what he sees is not important to him, but what he feels is important. In addition, it is possible that he is just comfortable in an environment that seems like a mess to the mother, chaos. After all, for him, it is not chaos, but in its own way an ordered environment, where he is easily oriented and feels better than in a room with an ideal order that seems cold and alien to him.

There are no such examples. Cases of misunderstanding between the most loving couples are not uncommon when an audial woman wants to hear affectionate words and declarations of love from a partner, while the visual partner believes that external signs of attention, such as gifts and flowers, are better than any words about love. You yourself can remember cases from your life when someone addressed you "in a foreign language" or you yourself did the same with another, saying to the audience or kinesthetic: "Can't you see?": "Don't you feel?" As a result, a scandal can even break out, which can be avoided if you understand in time that the other person is different and may not really feel, see or hear what seems to you self-evident, clear, obvious, understandable, and unquestionable.

You are already familiar with the characteristic features by which you can "calculate" a visual, audial, or kinesthetic. It is enough just to observe more closely the people with whom you often communicate in order to determine what type they are. Then just follow the tips on how to communicate with visuals, audials, and kinesthetics, and many problems and misunderstandings in your communication will be resolved by themselves.

How to communicate with visuals

Speak in their language, using such turns as "You see," "Look," "It's obvious," etc.

Frequently resort to communicating with visual images. If you want to interest them with a story, describe what you saw: color, size, and the shape of objects, visible features of the landscape and the appearance of people. It is even better to accompany the story with photographs, slides, video materials.

If you want to explain something to a visual, take a paper and a pencil and accompany your story with diagrams, a description of actions, a plan, etc.

Be understanding and appreciative of his love for picture books, comic books, visual arts, film, and theater.

Leave him little notes, write letters, postcards.

The visual will rejoice if you present him with a beautiful thing, as well as gifts that are beautifully decorated will not leave him indifferent.

How to communicate with audials

To speak their language, use the rhythm: "I listen to you," "Do you hear?", "Listen," etc.

Use hearing aids when talking about something: describe sounds, conversations, silence or noise, music, wind noise, birds singing, etc.

If you want to explain something to the audience, speak clearly, clearly, and expressively. Let your speech be rich in intonations, voice modulations. It is desirable that the movements of the head, hands, and the whole body match the rhythm of your voice - then your speech will sound more convincing for the auditorium.

Encourage his love of music; do not prevent his desire to remain in silence from time to time.

Give him compliments and good words, call more often, or leave voice messages.

An audial will be pleased with all the sounding gifts: audio equipment, audio recordings, watches with melodic combat or "wind music," as well as a ticket to a good concert.

How to communicate with kinesthetics

To speak with them in the same language, use the momentum: "Do you feel?", "It is extremely nice," "How do you relate it?" etc.

Use kinesthetic images if you want to interest kinesthetics with a story: talk about sensations (gentle warm waves, hot rays of the sun, fresh wind, facilities at the hotel, etc.).

If you want to explain something to kinesthetics, try to speak expressively and artistically, accompanying your speech with movement and gestures, play any situation in your faces so that he can feel and experience well what you are talking about.

Treat his love of comfort and comfort with understanding.

Touch him/her often, hug, communicate at a minimum distance. However, remember that there is kinesthetics who do not like the touches of strangers because this advice applies only to loved ones.

A kinesthetic will rejoice at any gift that promises pleasant sensations: for example, comfortable clothing, furniture, and interior items, bedding, cosmetics, perfume, body care products, equipment and equipment for sports and physical education, a subscription to a spa, a pool or on a massage trip to the resort.

Chapter 9. Determining your type of perception

Carefully read the following characteristics of visuals, audials, and kinesthetics and find out which of them are relevant to you.

If you are visual,

The visual first notes and remembers:

• details of the appearance and clothing of people

• the appearance of objects, things

• paints, colors, shades

• shapes and sizes

• the location of objects, the distance to them

• order or confusion

• beauty or ugliness

• movement and immobility

• the breadth of view, panorama

• clarity or blurry images

• brightness, lightness, or dimness

The visual often uses the words:

• watch

• see

• look

• appearance

• to look like

• notice

- portray
- demonstrate
- appear
- show
- display
- bright
- brilliant
- nice
- attractive
- to consider
- gloomy
- faded
- nondescript
- glow
- shine
- colorful
- transparent

Visual phrases
- I see the problem.
- Look at it from the other side.
- Glad to see your progress.
- This is some dark story.
- Clearly.
- This is an unseen case.
- Wait and see.

- Do not want to look at it.

- It is obvious.

- It is fundamentally needed to focus on the problem.

- On closer inspection...

- From point of view...

- In my opinion...

- Apparently...

- Do you see...

Features of appearance and behavior of the visual:

- expressive eyes
- attentive interested look
- head held high
- active mimicry
- restrained, mean gesticulation
- slightly constrained movements
- able to focus without being distracted by noise
- observant
- endowed with developed imagination

If you are audial

An audial first remembers:

- what people are talking about
- voice timbre
- speed and emotional nuances of speech
- correctness and incorrectness of speech, accent, dialect

- the volume of the sounds of the world
- tonality, tempo, the rhythm of sounds
- music, songs, melodies
- the place where the sound source is located, the distance to it
- the volume of sound
- harmonious or nonexistent

An audial often uses the words:
- quiet
- loud
- conversation
- speak
- chat
- questions
- tell
- listen
- consonant
- harmoniously
- discuss
- argue
- hint
- resonance
- shrill
- deafening
- to complain
- ringing

- noisy

- say yes

- pronounce

- euphonic

- silent

- silence

- voice

- sound

- rhythm

Audial-specific phrases

- I heard about it.

- You have not heard for a long time.

- This is unheard of the affair.

- I do not wish to listen and deal with this.

- All my ears buzzed about this.

- Everyone is talking about it.

- It sounds convincing.

- I missed it by the ears.

- I am listening really carefully.

- How you have not heard?

- The whole world has sounded the news.

- In truth…

- Word by word...

- Tell me…

- Have you heard about it?

Features of the appearance and behavior of the audial:

• habit to tilt your head slightly

• glance is often directed sideways or down

• has a habit of thinking out loud, talking to himself

• hardly concentrates in noisy environments

• loves silence

• gesturing, holding hands at chest level

• can shake his head, hand, foot or sway with his whole body to the beat of his own speech

• can both listen and talk

If you are kinesthetic

A kinesthetic first notices and remembers:

• warm or cold

• softness or hardness

• touches

• taste and smell

• bodily comfort or discomfort

• tension or relaxation

• heaviness or lightness

• movement or rest

• lethargy or activity

• stability or instability

A kinesthetic often uses the words:

- soft
- hard
- weighty
- light
- heavy
- move
- worry
- feel
- warm
- cold
- mood
- impression
- upset
- durable
- fascinating
- calm
- get annoyed
- injure
- touch
- comfortable
- flair
- touching

Kinesthetic phrases

- Here is a nice atmosphere.
- It hurt me a lot.
- I felt a warm attitude.
- It put me off balance.
- I caught the point.
- I support it.
- I don't move a finger for that.
- I'm very touched.
- We talked cordially.
- It shocked me.
- This is a hard question.
- Hard position.
- Cold reception.
- It is worn in the air.
- For my taste...
- I feel that...
- How to master...
- According to my feelings...

Features of appearance and behavior of kinesthetics:

• calm, relaxed

• often prone to corpulence

• actively gesticulates, usually holding hands at the level of the abdomen

• loves comfort, convenience

• it is most pleasant for him to communicate with a minimum distance from the interlocutor

• When communicating likes to touch the other person

• is mobile, restless

Chapter 10. Tests to determine your type of perception

et's turn to more accurate methods for determining your type of perception - namely, psychological tests. Three tests are suggested below. Go through them all, not necessarily in a row, you can in any order and at different times. This will allow you to get more reliable results, as well as help you in self-knowledge and reveal how objectively your self-image has been. But the most important thing is that testing will help you not only to identify which type of perception you have the most developed, but which of the three is less developed and which is very weak. This is important information that you will need in further work on the development of intelligence to properly rewire your mind.

Test 1

Evaluate whether or not you agree with each of the following statements. If you agree, put a "+" (plus) sign next to the corresponding approval number, if you do not agree, put a "-" (minus) sign. It is necessary to answer quickly, without hesitation.

1. I remember well everything that occurs on my way to work, and I can reproduce the smallest details in my memory.

2. I often find myself humming something under my breath.

3. I prefer clothes in which I feel comfortable and never sacrifice comfort for the sake of fashion.

4. I enjoy water treatments, visiting the SPA-salon, steam bath, and sauna.

5. The color of the walls in my house, the color scheme of the interior, the color of the car is very important to me.

6. I can easily determine by steps which of my family walks along the corridor, enters a house or a room.

7. Often I copy the way other people speak, for fun, I imitate their voices.

8. For me it is very important how I look. I pay a lot of attention to my appearance.

9. Periodically taking massage is for me both a necessity and a pleasure.

10. I have a good memory for faces - if I have ever seen a person, I will remember him even after many years.

11. I like to dance, exercise and sport.

12. In the clothing store, I immediately see which item suits me and which one does not.

13. When I hear music that was popular during my childhood and adolescence, it immediately seemed to be transferred there.

14. At every opportunity (in transport, queues, during meals) I either read or watch the news, or watch a video on the Internet.

15. I like to talk on the phone, I do it often and for a long time.

16. I have to control my weight due to the tendency to be overweight.

17. I like listening to audiobooks or literary works performed by actors over the radio more than reading ordinary books myself.

18. If I get tired, I feel the tension in my whole body.

19. I love to take pictures.

20. I remember well what other people say to me; I can reproduce it word for word.

21. I love flowers and beautiful natural landscapes.

22. It is very important to me that the house be warm, cozy, and comfortable.

23. I use the diary, where I write down everything that I have to do.

24. I often say my thoughts out loud, even if no one hears me.

25. Long trips in transport usually tire me out.

26. The impression that a person makes on me depends on the timbre of his voice.

27. I always pay attention to how a person with whom he has to communicate is dressed.

28. In the morning, before you get up, it is important for me how to stretch and stretch.

29. I can only sleep properly if the bed is comfortable for me.

30. I find it difficult to find shoes that would be really comfortable.

31. I enjoy any shows; I love theater, cinema, and entertainment programs on television.

32. I like to look at strangers, to notice how they look, what they wear, how they behave, to determine their age, mood.

33. I love the sound of rain, birds singing, the sound of the wind, the sea surf.

34. In conversation, I can listen and hear the other person.

35. During the day, I am often drawn to warm up, move, and if there is no such opportunity, then I feel bad.

36. The slightest noise can prevent me from falling asleep - even the sound of a ticking alarm clock.

37. I like to listen to music, and it is important for me that it sounds in a good performance or in a good quality recording.

38. I cannot sit still when the music sounds; I begin either to beat the time with my foot or to dance.

39. I love traveling, trips, excursions, where you can see many new places and attractions.

40. I love that all things at home and in the workplace lay strictly in their places.

41. I love clothes and linens from soft, pleasantly natural fabrics adjacent to the body.

42. The lighting in the house is very important to be - the general atmosphere of comfort or lack of it depends on the sources of light.

43. If I am offered to go to a museum, to a cinema or to a concert, I would prefer a concert.

44. The way a person shakes my hand says a lot about him.

45. I love to visit museums and exhibitions.

46. I like to participate in discussions where you can exchange views, and maybe even argue.

47. Touching can tell me more than words.

48. I need silence to do work that requires concentration.

Processing results

Count all the advantages that you put in paragraphs 1, 5, 8, 10, 12, 14, 19, 21, 23, 27, 31, 32, 39, 40, 42, 45.

If there are eight-plus points, you are visual.

Count all the advantages that you put in paragraphs 2, 6, 7, 13, 15, 17, 20, 24, 26, 33, 34, 36, 37, 43, 46, 48.

If eight or more pluses - you audial.

Count all the advantages that you put in paragraphs 3, 4, 9, 11, 16, 18, 22, 25, 28, 29, 30, 35, 38, 41, 44, 47.

If there are eight or more pros, you are kinesthetic. Now compare the number of pulses in each of the three groups. The one in which they are most reflected is your most active way of perceiving. The one in which there are fewer, but more than eight, reflects your second-degree perception type. The one in which there are less than eight reflects your "weak link" - the least developed type of perception.

It may happen that in two of the three groups you get about the same number of advantages. This means that you have not one, but two types of perception are basic and are developed approximately equally.

If you have approximately the same number of advantages in all three groups, then all types of perception are developed evenly. True, this happens very rarely and usually happens in people who have already specifically engaged in the development of their visual, auditory, and kinesthetic abilities.

Test 2

In each of the three groups of statements in front of each of them, put a score from 1 to 5, where 1 - "It does not concern me", 2 - "Very rarely, but it happens", 3 - "Sometimes it happens", 4 - "Pretty often ", 5 -" Almost always. "

Group 1

1. I remember the information better if I write it down right away.

2. During the study, I conduct very detailed notes.

3. Reading a book, I mentally imagine pictures and images, like in a movie.

4. The best way to get information for me is video, movies or TV shows.

5. In order to master the new technique, I, first, am acquainted with the instruction.

6. The best instruction for me is the one where there are illustrations, graphic material.

7. It is easier for me to communicate personally than by telephone - when I see a person, I understand better what he is saying.

8. I am not interested in lectures and reports if they are not accompanied by visual material.

9. I remember people's faces well, but I don't remember names well.

10. I'd rather remember the name if I read it (for example, on a business card or a badge).

Group 2

1. I'd rather remember any information if I retell it to someone.

2. I prefer to get knowledge from lectures, rather than from books.

3. I will do a better job if they talk to me and tell me in detail what my task is.

4. Any extraneous sound prevents me from thinking.

5. I like quiet, calm music.

6. It is easier for me to communicate by phone than personally - the appearance of the interlocutor does not distract from the meaning of his words.

7. I remember the names well, but I do not remember the faces.

8. I have a good memory for jokes and riddles.

9. I remember the voices well, I recognize the artists by their voice, even looking at the screen, and I can accurately determine who is calling, even if I have not seen or heard a person for a long time.

10. I cannot watch not the TV screen, but only listen to understand the movie or TV show.

Group 3

1. I master the new technique in practice, very rarely referring to the instructions.

2. In work, I need breaks to warm up.

3. I do not like monotony; I need a frequent change of environment or type of activity.

4. Whenever possible, I prefer to settle in a more comfortable posture.

5. It is very hard for me to remain still for a long time.

6. I have a habit of swinging my foot or tapping my fingers, pulling my hair, turning a pen in my hands, etc.

7. In the museum, I always want to touch everything with my hands.

8. I am rather active in gesturing.

9. If I like the other person, I want to move closer to him.

10. Listening to a lecture and a report, I draw all sorts of scribbles in a notebook.

Processing results

Count the number of points in each group. If the maximum result is in group 1 is you are visual, in group 2 it is audial, in group 3 it is kinesthetic. Then reveal which type of perception is developed to a lesser extent and which is very weak.

Test 3

Of the three answers to each question, choose the one that is closer to you, without wasting time thinking.

1. You have to do something new for yourself with your own hands - for example, to assemble furniture, to sew something, to plant a tree, etc. In what way would you prefer to act?

A. Read about how this is done.

B. Ask knowledgeable people - let them tell.

C. You will figure it out yourself, comprehend the matter immediately in practice by trial and error.

2. You came to the library to take a book with you on vacation - it should be the most pleasant, easy reading. What will you choose?

A. Travel notes with illustrations.

B. Psychological detective or melodrama.

C. The book about proper nutrition and a healthy lifestyle.

3. You write an article, report, or letter and find that you are not sure of the correct spelling of a word. There is no dictionary at hand. How will you behave?

A. Write the word in different variants and in appearance, you will try to determine which one is correct.

B. You will say the word out loud, thinking about how it is written.

C. Write the option that intuitively seems right to you.

4. You visited a new company of people. What do you remember first when you leave?

A. The faces of the people, the way they are dressed, but not the names.

B. Names of people, but not faces and not clothes.

C. The overall atmosphere and how you felt.

5. You will have an exam. How will you prepare?

A. Read the textbook and notes, trying to remember as much as possible.

B. Retell the material you have learned aloud.

C. Write short cheat sheets on cards that can be hung on the walls and studied on the go.

6. Imagine that in front of you is a large white sheet of paper on which "apple" is written large. What is your first reaction?

A. You have presented what an apple looks like.

B. You introduced the word "apple."

C. You felt the taste and smell of an apple.

7. You need to focus, concentrate, mobilize your mental abilities, and solve some difficult task. What can hinder you the most?

A. The picture on the TV screen, even if the sound is turned off.

B. The sound of a working TV or other noise.

C. Inconvenient posture or too tight clothes, shoes.

8. You find yourself in a situation of forced waiting - for example, in a queue for an appointment with an official. How do you behave?

A. Look at your surroundings, watch people.

B. Enter into a conversation with others or have some kind of mental dialogue with yourself.

C. Pull something in your hands, trample or walk back and forth.

9. You came to the exhibition. What method of inspection do you like more?

A. First, read the description of the exhibition, then each picture and consider them all in order.

B. Take advantage of the audio guide or join the tour.

C. To walk from picture to picture without any plan - "where the legs will bring."

10. Someone behaved, in your opinion, unworthy. What will you do?

A. With all of your appearance, and above all with your expression, you will demonstrate your disapproval and condemnation.

B. Say what you think about this.

C. Demonstratively leave, or maybe knock your fist on the table or slam the door loudly.

11. Someone told you very good news. How will you respond?

A. Smile, your eyes will shine with joy.

B. Say a monologue on how you are excited.

C. Hop up and clap your hands.

12. You heard a song that you like. What are you doing?

A. Visibly imagine what is sung in it.

B. Sing along.

C. Dance or beat off the rhythm with your foot.

13. Some interesting story has happened to you. You want to share it with others. How would you do it best?

A. Would write about it.

B. Told orally.

C. Played in the faces.

14. Imagine that you were invited to a restaurant and you were completely satisfied with the proposed menu, but still you did not like it there. Why?

A. There was a tasteless interior.

B. The singer had an unpleasant voice.

C. It was stuffy, hot or cold, or uncomfortable chairs, tables.

Processing results

Calculate how many answers you have A, how many B and how many B. If A dominates the answers, you are visual, B is audial, and C is kinesthetic. Accordingly, by the number of answers, you can determine which type of perception you have in second place, and which type in third.

Conclusion

What if different tests in Chapter 10 showed different results? Perhaps you have not quite objectively answered some questions. In this case, focus on those two tests out of three, which gave similar indicators. Thus, you will get a fairly accurate answer about the most characteristic types of perception for you. Namely, you will determine that you have three sensory channels, of which:

• one channel - the one you use most often;

• the second channel is the one that you use only occasionally;

• the third channel is one that you use very rarely or never use at all.

The truth is that you receive all three types of signals from the outside world — visual, auditory, and kinesthetic, but the brain receives complete information only from one of these types of signals. The rest are completely or partially ignored by your mind.

Further work on the book will help you correct this situation.

This is the basis of rewiring the mind. Funny, humans hardly ever know what they are not taught. Understanding the basics of who you are, only then can you actively develop yourself and be a positive influence to yourself and to others around you!

CPSIA information can be obtained
at www.ICGtesting.com
Printed in the USA
LVHW080344020421
683209LV00003B/352

9 781802 345742